PRAISE FOR
ASCENT FROM DARKNESS

"God's power to transform a life never ceases to amaze me. Michael Leehan's gripping story from darkness to light will move you, challenge you, inspire you, and change you."

CRAIG GROESCHEL
SENIOR PASTOR, LIFECHURCH.TV
AUTHOR, *THE CHRISTIAN ATHEIST*

"Through the years I have been privileged to hear the amazing stories of people the Lord has set free from all manner of bondage, but none are more compelling than the story of God's power as demonstrated through the life of Michael Leehan. Because I have found freedom from my own bondage, and because I found great encouragement in the midst of my own struggle for freedom through reading the stories of other overcomers, I highly recommend *Ascent from Darkness* to you."

DENNIS JERNIGAN
WORSHIP LEADER AND SONGWRITER, *YOU ARE MY ALL IN ALL*
AUTHOR, *GIANT KILLERS*

"Truth is better than fiction, as the saying goes, and that's an understatement in regards to Michael's story. I can honestly say what you will read here will open your eyes not only to a reality our general public knows very little about, but also to the Glory of God in the life of a modern day Saul of Tarsus/Paul! Well done, Michael! Your past doesn't hold a candle to your present."

ALICE WELLINGTON, PhD

PSYCHOLOGIST

"Mike's story will make you weep and laugh, set you free, and transform your soul! You have to read it now!"

CHRIS SPRADLIN

PASTOR, EUZOA, STEAMBOAT SPRINGS

COFOUNDER, EPICPARENT.TV

"*Ascent from Darkness* is the most compelling story of God's power over evil you will read. I know this because I have personally witnessed Michael's transformation from death to life. This book will build your faith and grow your love not for a man, but for a God who still chases after those who are lost."

CHRIS BEALL

OKC CAMPUS PASTOR, LIFECHURCH.TV

"I believe this man is a modern day Paul. His story has changed the way I see the power of God. I have been given the opportunity to spend three days a week having coffee with the guy and would consider him to be one of my closest friends. I have watched God do so much in his life in such a short time. If this book doesn't help you see the reality of the spiritual realm, then I am not sure what will. I pray that the spirit of God will speak to you and open you up in a whole new way to what God wants to do with your life."

KETRIC NEWELL

YOUTH PASTOR, CROSSPOINT.TV

ASCENT FROM DARKNESS

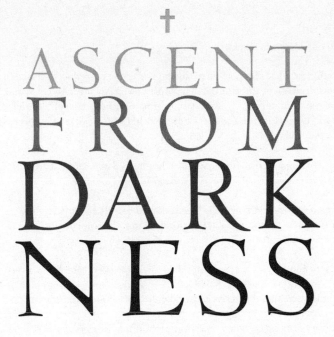

ASCENT FROM DARK NESS

HOW SATAN'S SOLDIER
BECAME GOD'S WARRIOR

A TRUE STORY

MICHAEL LEEHAN

✝

THOMAS NELSON
Since 1798

NASHVILLE   DALLAS   MEXICO CITY   RIO DE JANEIRO

Published in Nashville, Tennessee, by Thomas Nelson. Thomas Nelson is a registered trademark of Thomas Nelson, Inc.

Thomas Nelson, Inc., titles may be purchased in bulk for educational, business, fund-raising, or sales promotional use. For information, please e-mail SpecialMarkets@ThomasNelson.com.

Scripture quotations are taken from the Holy Bible, New International Version®, NIV®. Copyright © 1973, 1978, 1984, 2011 by Biblica, Inc.™ Used by permission of Zondervan. All rights reserved worldwide. www.zondervan.com.

This story is based on true events, but certain names, persons, characters, places, and dates have been changed so that the persons and characters portrayed bear no resemblance to persons actually living or dead.

Page design by Mark L. Mabry

Library of Congress Cataloging-in-Publication Data

Leehan, Michael, 1956-
  Ascent from darkness : how Satan's soldier became God's warrior : a true story / Michael Leehan.
    p. cm.
  ISBN 978-0-8499-4703-2 (trade paper)
  1. Leehan, Michael, 1956- 2. Christian converts--United States--Biography.
3. Satanism. I. Title.
  BV4935.L365A3 2011
  248.2'46092--dc22
  [B]

                                         2011016008

Printed in the United States of America

11 12 13 14 QG 5 4 3 2 1

To those who struggle and strive to get through each day in a world that seems detached and broken

CONTENTS

ACKNOWLEDGMENTS

*A*scent from Darkness was not an easy book to write, especially since it is my first. Countless hours and months sitting in a chair, on a beach, in a park, or in one of the many other places to write this book was not something I would have ever thought I could do, especially with my personality and aversion to sitting still. If not for the professionals who came into my life to help guide me through the process, *Ascent from Darkness* would have never come to fruition.

It is with a humble and grateful heart that I thank Brian Sanders, David Reiner, Debbie Wickwire, and Jennifer Stair for their expertise and godly guidance and prayers during the arduous task of completing this book. I want to also thank Chang and staff at All About Cha Stylish Tea and Coffee for allowing me to sit in their booths for months on end, writing.

With tearful eyes, I want to thank God for His Son and pursuit of me, for His love of me. I give Him this book and my life. Without His guidance and direction in this project and in the lives of everyone involved, *Ascent from Darkness* would not have been possible.

Marisa Ann, Kristin Nicole, Jason David, my three wonderful children; thank you for the love you have for your father. Thank you for your endurance and support.

AUTHOR'S NOTE

Everything stated in this book is true. I'm not going to lie or stretch the truth in order to impress you. I do not desire to make my experiences seem better or worse than they actually were. My goal is to tell the truth about my dark and torturous journey into satanism and how the Lord spared me from a tragic ending. All I can do is testify to His work during this process.

I am not a biblical scholar, a seminary graduate, or a professional writer. I am not an expert on any denomination, cult, or religion. I am a person who has placed his faith in Jesus Christ and His promises for all believers. I am a flawed man who has seen God's marvelous light and, by His grace and mercy, has literally been given a second chance at life. I'm simply here to share my story of what God did for me and continues to do in my life.

Undoubtedly, many will question the spiritual issues raised in a book that discusses satanism. That's to be expected. But let me be clear about this: I am now a child of the Most High God. My faith in Jesus Christ isn't open for debate.

Ascent from Darkness addresses issues pertaining to hopelessness, depression, mental illness, spiritual warfare, incarceration, addictions, and many other struggles with which you or someone else you may know may be afflicted. My intent in writing this book is to shed God's light into these dark circumstances and to give hope to those who feel hopeless.

I pray that this book will help set captives free through the light of our wonderful and loving God.

CHAPTER 1

THE EARLY YEARS

For we are God's handiwork, created in Christ Jesus to do good works, which God prepared in advance for us to do.

—EPHESIANS 2:10

January 12, 1976
Edmond, Oklahoma

My best friend, Eldon Felch, had an apartment a few miles from my work, so when I got off around 5 p.m., I headed over to his place to hang out and knock back a few beers. I had four hours to kill before Eldon got back from his job at a local grocery store, so I did what many other nineteen-year-old boys would do: I polished off a six-pack. Waiting until 9 p.m. for Eldon to show up seemed like an eternity, so I walked down to a local 7-Eleven to pick up another six-pack.

As I walked to the store, pain began shooting up my left knee. I'd injured my knee playing football in a sandlot game, and my knee was wrecked. I'd had three surgeries already and needed another, so I had a bottle of pain meds handy. Popping pills to manage the pain in my bad knee had become routine; I had been doing so for about two years now.

I must have looked older, or the cashiers didn't really care, since neither of the attendants working that night asked for my ID. I took my purchased six-pack, left the store, and walked back to Eldon's apartment. The frigid January weather didn't help my aching knee one bit, so when I got back to Eldon's, I popped three pills—a full day's dosage—and washed it down with a fresh Budweiser.

I opened the last beer in my second six-pack around 8 p.m. and contemplated another trip to 7-Eleven. I checked my stash of pain pills and noticed I had ten pills left. I popped two more to brace myself for the long walk and the frigid night air. I lingered, sipping my last beer, waiting for the pills to kick in. My knee hurt, but the pain I was most trying to dull was the emotional pain of a recent breakup with a girl I was in love with.

Still lying on the couch, I took my last sip of beer. When I reached for my bottle of pills, it was empty. *I don't remember taking those*, I thought.

I tried to get up, but my legs felt heavy. I lay back on the tan couch and looked around the room. The TV was on, but I didn't hear the sound coming from it. A river of warmth rushed through me, and everything began to slow down. *Better get up*, I told myself. But when I tried to move, my feet were cinder blocks. My hands tingled, my face felt flushed, my heart raced, and I began to sweat. *This is not good*, I thought. I was in trouble, and I knew it.

I started to panic. I somehow mustered the strength to move off the couch but fell flat on the floor. I rolled on my side and tried to get to the phone on the kitchen wall. I needed help. I wanted to shout, but I had no voice. My head was clouded, and I struggled to breathe. But I had to get to the phone. I crawled a few feet, collapsed, then passed out.

When I came to a short time later, the room felt bitterly cold, but I still felt sweat gathering on my body. All my bodily systems were in overdrive, and I knew I didn't have long. I made it up on all fours, then to one knee, and began to stretch my hand up the wall. But, inches from the phone, I gave out and slid down the wall and lay facedown on the linoleum. I rolled over and stared at the ceiling. The room spun, my stomach churned, my heart was beating in my head, and my shirt was drenched. My body began to twitch uncontrollably. With rapid stomach contractions I gasped for air, struggling to breathe. Then the room went dark.

Scenes flashed through my head. I saw myself clearly as a five-year-old playing in my family's yard and talking with our neighbors, whose kind faces were lit by the brightness of the California sun. I recognized my mother and father, but they were moving away from me, and I couldn't see their faces. I wanted to call to them, but they were distant and out of reach.

Then I was at the beach, and I saw the face of an angry adult whaling on me for some unforgivable mistake. She held me under the salt-filled water until I took my last breath. I saw my tears and my fear and my helplessness.

I saw myself crying every night as I lay down to sleep. As a child, I had prayed to two statues, one of Mary and the other of Jesus, that were situated on my headboard. I prayed that they would rescue me from a life of fear and desperation I already found unbearable and from the emotions of fear and desperation that were too weighty for any child. I pleaded with the statues in the simple words of a brokenhearted child who just wanted relief. But relief never came. The statue of the sweet-faced woman, who I was told had the power to help me, did not. My cries went unheeded. The gentle smile of the man statue seemed to be laughing at me. I was alone and abandoned. One night after praying, I broke the heads off the two plastic statues, went to the backyard, and buried them in the soil of a nearby garden.

The next thing I saw was my body lying in an ambulance as it roared down Danforth Road on its way to Edmond Medical Center. I floated high outside the vehicle and saw the commotion that was going on inside as the medics attended to me. I saw the oxygen mask on my face and my shirt torn back as I lay unconscious on the white transport gurney. I watched my body jerk when paddles were put on my chest to jump-start me back to the world I'd just exited. But I didn't want to go back to the pain, to the confusion, to the loneliness and isolation. I saw fear on the medics' faces as my life began to slip away from them. Watching this scene, all I could think was, *Good. It is over.*

Then I heard a voice say to me, *"Not yet, son. I have too much for you to do!"*

I fell back asleep.

✝

I opened my eyes to a dimly lit room. I was covered with a white sheet and a thin blanket. *Am I alive? Where am I?* I didn't know the day or time, and I don't think I could recall my name. Thoughts came to me so slowly. It was as if my circuits had been jammed and the synapses weren't firing. I felt a crushing fatigue as I tried to move my legs.

The back of my left hand had a tube inserted into it and white cloth tape bundled around it. There were electrodes attached to my chest on one end and to a monitor on the other. The room was warm and empty, save for a bouquet of flowers on my bedside table and a few get-well cards on the windowsill. I closed my eyes to rest. I had no strength. *I'm alive . . . but why?*

"Michael, when are you going to come back to us?" I heard a gentle voice whisper. My eyes opened slowly, and I saw a young nurse changing my IV bag. The clock on the wall showed 2 a.m. The nurse had her back to me when in a raspy voice I asked, "Where am I?"

The nurse turned on her heels. "Oh, thank God!"

With tears in her eyes, she took my hand and held it warmly. She tried to get me to talk, but I had no energy. I tried to go back to sleep, but she kept talking to me and told me to stay with her. Then I heard her yell out for assistance.

I wanted to sleep so badly. My eyes closed. She shook me, calling my name over and over.

Then I heard another woman in the room. She asked the nurse, "Are you sure? It's okay. Let him sleep. Call the doctor on duty."

I heard a man's voice call my name. A bright light shone into my left eye as a hand forced open my eyelid. I tried to pull away. "Can I please get some sleep?" I muttered.

The unfamiliar doctor sternly said, "Michael, you need to wake up."

I struggled against waking because I was totally drained, but the doctor continued. "Michael, you need to stay with me. You've got to fight."

Through bleary eyes I looked at the doctor and was blinded by the large ceiling lights. I winced and shut my eyes.

A little confused and combative, I blurted, "Please turn those off." As the nurse dimmed the lights, I pushed myself up in the bed and then fell backward. Someone gently lifted my head and shoulders up as another placed pillows behind me.

The doctor asked me how I felt and asked if I was in pain. I told him I felt as if I had been hit by a truck, I was so sore. I asked him what had happened to me. Instead of answering my question, he asked me what my name was, who the president of the United States was, and what year I was born. I told him my name, but that was all I could remember. Tired of his questions, I pleaded, "Can I please just go back to sleep?"

"Sure," he replied. "Push this button in your right hand if you need anything, and your family physician will be in to see you shortly."

Again I woke to probing questions and yet another physical examination. My eyes opened fully this time to sunshine peering through the window. I felt much more awake and coherent than the night before. I heard the familiar voice of my mother saying, "Son, you scared me. Oh, I'm glad you came back to us!"

I turned to my right and saw my mother by my side. I looked behind her and saw Father Frances, the Catholic priest from her church. He greeted me and said he was so glad I woke up, that I had pulled a stupid stunt but God had forgiven me. My mom later revealed that Father Frances had given me the sacrament of last rites while I was unconscious. She told me that when I arrived at the hospital, my lips were blue and my skin was cold as medics rushed me on a gurney to the emergency room. She was sure she would never see me alive again.

✝

Two weeks later, I stared out the window of the hospital that had been my home for the past month, overlooking the city several stories below. It was mid-February, and snow covered the streets and sat in large drifts by the roadside. It appeared to have snowed for months.

I heard a man say, "It was one of the worst snowstorms we've ever seen." I turned away from the window and saw my new doctor approach me.

"How are you feeling?" he asked.

I looked around the room, then back at the doctor.

"Good," I replied.

He looked at me curiously. "Was your overdose intentional?"

I answered, "I don't remember much of that night, Doc, other than being outside and then above the ambulance. I do remember being glad that I was somewhere else. I felt lighter. I felt somewhat at ease. I wanted to be out of this world and to stay in that place, wherever that was."

I paused, wondering if I could confide in him. "I also heard a voice, Doc."

He raised an eyebrow. "Oh? What did the voice say?"

"It was a male voice, maybe my dad. I don't know. He said, 'Not yet, son. I have too much for you to do.'"

The doctor scribbled something on my chart and then answered, "That was just your imagination."

✝

A few hours later, I was riding in a car with my mom. We were headed home, my mind still muddled from an event that was now a month old, when my mom asked, "How do you feel?"

"I'm good," I said, tired of people asking me that question.

"The doctor said to keep an eye on you. He's not convinced you didn't try to kill yourself, son. Did you?"

"No."

"Dad is pretty upset, but I wouldn't tell him much. You know he doesn't know how to handle such things."

"Don't worry, Mom," I said. "I know how Dad is."

In my mind I cursed him. *What a wuss! Dad is such a coward; he can't face any kind of emotional conflict. He can't even say "I love you" to his son who nearly died. He can't go to a hospital because it is too clean, too sterile. He fears doctors, fears women, fears conflict. He only thinks about himself. Don't think of your son, Dad! It might hurt too much!*

Determined not to stick around the house long enough to talk to my father, I said, "I'm going to see Carol when I get home. Is my car still at the house?"

"Son," my mother said gently, "Carol broke up with you the day you went to the hospital."

"She did?"

My thoughts jumped to the last time I had seen Carol. We were intimate and sharing conversation. I walked out of her parents' house and was headed to work. Wait—did I? She was concerned about something. Why was she crying? My memory refused to stay still. I tried to remember the details of our last day together, but every time I pinned something down, another memory popped up and I had to rethink the whole situation.

My mom's response shook me from my thoughts. "Yes, and you need to stay away from her. She's too young and doesn't know what she wants yet."

My mind started to once again whirl with justifications for everything behind my mother's heavy words.

Ah . . . Mom just believes that because she thinks Carol is responsible for my overdose. She doesn't even know Carol. Carol knows what she wants. She's seventeen! . . . Parents. Dad couldn't care less, and Mom pretends she does. All Mom cares about is herself—her gambling at the bingo hall, her smokes, and her controlling dad. How does she know what Carol wants? She's rarely even talked to Carol!

My mother pulled the car into the driveway of our small bungalow-style house. I noticed the yard still had melting piles of dirty snow spotting the yard and driveway. I glanced up and saw my dad open the front door and stand behind the glass storm door, awaiting my arrival. The morning sun pierced through the door and illuminated the can of Coors he was holding. It wasn't even noon yet.

"I need one of those pain pills the doc gave me, Mom."

"It's not time," she replied. "He said to not let you have another one till 2 p.m."

"Come on," I urged. "It's okay, Mom. One pill won't kill me. I have a bad headache."

After a sigh, my mom handed me the bottle. "Son, you are nineteen years old. I'm not going to treat you like a baby . . . Here!"

"Thanks. I'm going to the car wash. See ya in a while."

"Aren't you going in to see your father? Besides, the doctor said you should take it easy for at least three or four days, so I'm not sure it's safe for you to drive. You were out of it for nearly two weeks and in the hospital for a month," she reminded me. "And remember, you have an appointment with your psychiatrist on Thursday. He wants to see you twice a week until he feels you are okay."

"Mom! I am in great shape. I just want to go somewhere, anywhere but here." I could feel anger rising in me as I continued. "I hate shrinks anyway. They don't know what they are doing. Dr.

Knox is an idiot; I only tell him what he wants to hear. Forget him, Mom . . . Forget this whole freakin' world! Why do you care, anyway? You never care about anything but yourself!"

I hardly had time to realize what was coming out of my mouth. My mom didn't respond to my outburst. She reached for the door and calmly said, "Well, I think you need to take it slowly. You need to get back into the groove. And you have to get back to work. Your grandmother called yesterday and said your job at LongBell is still there for you." LongBell Lumber was a local lumberyard where my grandmother had worked for more than forty years. When I moved from California to Oklahoma, she helped me secure a job there as a delivery truck driver.

"I'm sorry, Mom. I'm just a little agitated. I'm not a baby and am tired of the doctors and everyone treating me like one . . . This medicine makes me weird too. It's hard to think and talk. It's like it's slowing my mind down. Weird stuff, Mom."

"Well, the doctor said it can make you drowsy. That's probably what's happening, son."

"No, I'm not just drowsy. It's like I can't even think. I can't explain it. I feel like I'm not *me* anymore."

I reached around slowly and got a couple of bags from the backseat, a clear jug to urinate in—*why did she bring that home?*—the release papers from the hospital, a prescription, and some get-well cards. After gathering my stuff, I opened the door of the car and headed toward the front door. My legs felt weak. I still could not think clearly. It was as if my thoughts were not mine. I was thinking differently . . . so slowly. It took longer to take in my surroundings. My mind seemed detached from my senses. I tried to walk the steps leading up to the door, but I stumbled. My mind was out of sync with my legs. *It must be the drugs*, I thought.

My dad swung open the storm door for me and said, "Hey, son."

"Hey, Dad. Man, you're getting old. Your beard sure is white. It looks like you haven't shaven in a few weeks."

Surely he knows I'm joking, but he does look awful . . . Why the heck am I so foggy? My mouth is so dry . . . I'm thirsty. I gotta get out of here.

Trying to shake off my thoughts, I asked, "Anyway, why didn't you come see me, Dad?"

"You know I don't like hospitals," he said.

I looked around the filthy house. This was typical—dust and dirt everywhere and everything out of place. The green shag carpet looked as if it hadn't been vacuumed in the past month. The white ceilings were stained with nicotine. The small kitchen had dishes on every counter. The dining room table was piled with clutter. Exasperated, I threw my bags on the floor.

"Are hospitals too clean, Dad? Is that your problem? What is it about chaos that you like? I had this place spotless, and now look at it!" I sighed. "I have to go."

"Where you headed off to?"

"It doesn't matter." I paused, wanting to ask him something but not sure I wanted to hear the answer. "Dad, I have a question for you."

"Okay," he muttered.

"Were you in the ambulance with me?"

He took a long drink from his beer can before answering. "No."

Why did I just ask that? Of course he wasn't there. When has Dad ever been there when I needed him? He just hides whenever there's a problem.

"I'm outta here," I said. "I'm going to the car wash and then to see Eldon."

I jumped in my car and drove to try to clear my mind. Finally alone—no doctors, no nurses, no family—I was free to think. My driving instincts took over as soon as I turned the key in the ignition, but my senses still seemed to lag behind.

Whoa, I better be careful. I've driven drunk before, but this is a trip. These meds have got to go . . . I can't think with this stuff in me. I don't want to run over someone.

My thoughts drifted to the voice I had heard during the ambulance ride, when I felt like I was somewhere else. *Where did that voice come from? It was so comforting, so reassuring. It sounded—or felt—a little like my dad, but it wasn't him . . . Who told me that he had so much for me to do? Such a calm and gentle voice. It was so clean, so pure . . . Was it real?* I shook my head, trying to clear my thoughts as I continued to drive. *Whatever . . . The doc was right. It was just my imagination.*

I arrived in the parking lot of the grocery store where my buddy Eldon worked. I entered the store and saw Eldon stocking a shelf.

"Hey dude, looks like you're working too hard," I said.

Eldon turned and saw me. "Hey, Mike! I'm so glad you are okay! How do you feel? I came to the hospital every day when you were out . . . You scared the heck out of me. What were you thinking?"

As my head lowered, I responded, "I'm not sure what was going on that night. I was just gonna get drunk before we went out."

Eldon said, "Mike, what was going on that night was Carol! You must have been upset about it. Let her go, man."

"I have," I responded quickly. "At least, I think I have . . ."

Eldon nodded. "I've been there, bud."

Talking about Carol was painful, so I decided to change the

subject. "You want to go to Scorpio's tonight?" Scorpio's was a local seedy dancing bar.

"Think that's a good idea, man?" Eldon asked.

"I think it's a perfect idea. It's like you said: I gotta let her go and move on."

"Okay, man . . . but I don't think we should stay out too late. I'll pick you up at six."

✝

My life continued to be shallow and without much direction. I hid my emotions behind prescription drugs and alcohol. Even the near-death experience didn't change me much. I saw myself as a bulletproof nineteen-year-old always living on the edge.

The rest of the year carried on much the same, with partying, dating local girls, and working at the lumberyard. I was fully recovered and back to my normal lifestyle.

In February, one year after my accidental overdose, I found a source of new inspiration when I met a girl whom I began to have a lot of fun with. Amber was great, beautiful, and into water-skiing—a passion I picked up in my childhood. Now that I lived in Oklahoma where there were lakes in abundance, I water-skied a lot.

I had finally moved out of my parents' house and was living in an apartment with a buddy who worked with me at LongBell Lumber Company. The building industry was booming. This meant the business at LongBell increased substantially. Back then, there were no home-improvement stores like Home Depot or Lowe's, so builders relied solely on local lumberyards. I delivered lumber twelve hours per day and on weekends helped my dad refurbish the home he and Mom lived in.

One hot Saturday in June, I was at my father's house, installing an attic ventilation system to ease the attic heat. It was well over ninety degrees outside, and the attic I was in was much hotter. As I worked in the sweltering attic, I was thinking of my girlfriend and trying to finish the project so we could go waterskiing as we had planned. Although I had only known Amber for four months, we were planning to be married in July.

I was in a hurry to get done. I was overheated; I had been in the extreme heat for a half hour and was past the point of sweating. I felt light-headed.

The exit from the attic was through a two-by-four-foot opening nine feet above the concrete floor. I had placed a stepladder below to gain entrance; there was no built-in ladder. The air-conditioned flow of air rushed through the opening and enticed me to hurry even more to get cooled down.

About four feet from the opening was a framing brace situated on top of one of the ceiling joists. In my hurry to get out of the hot attic, I tripped on the brace and was thrust headfirst through the opening and toward the concrete below. Seven feet below the ceiling, my right arm slightly hit the side of the washing machine and was pushed backward, not allowing me to protect my head from the inevitable collision with the floor. The left side of my forehead impacted the concrete with a loud thud. The next memory I had was waking up in a hospital bed a few days later.

According to my mom, on the day of my fall, she and my dad had left the house for a few hours to go shopping. She said she had yelled up in the attic to tell me they were leaving and I told her I was almost done and would call her later in the day. When they got home four hours later, Mom called out to her dog, to feed her.

She couldn't find Mia (her small poodle), but when she ventured into the washroom, Mia was licking vomit and blood from my face. I had been unconscious for at least three hours. She told me I was lying in a pool of blood and did not wake up when she shook me, so she called an ambulance.

†⊦

When I woke up in the hospital room, I could not see out of my left eye; it was swollen shut. I had several stitches above it. I could barely see out of my swollen right eye but saw enough to notice a nurse by my side. A few moments later a doctor came in and spoke with me. I was groggy but coherent. I answered the questions he had for me. I was hurting. My neck hurt, my shoulder hurt, and my head hurt. The medication I was on helped numb the pain that was normal with the type of injury I sustained.

A few days later, after many CT scans and tests to determine the extent of my injuries, I was released from the hospital. Surprisingly, it appeared my fall would have no life-threatening or long-term effects on my health. The doctors told me that possible repercussions were years down the line and may involve epilepsy or many other effects from the blow to my body, but for now, everything was peculiarly clear. They were surprised that I survived the blow with just a concussion, contusions, a dislocated right shoulder, and a skull fracture. According to the experts, my age, vigor, and strong disposition were key factors in my recuperation from the fall.

Three weeks later I returned to work. Four weeks later I married my future children's mother.

✝

Amber and I were in love, and as newlyweds we did everything together: water-skiing, antique shopping, home improvement projects, and the list goes on. Our marriage produced a lot of joy at first. However, within a relatively short time, our relationship began a downward spiral. Both my wife and I had short tempers. With a poor support system on both sides of our family and no real foundation to build upon, our marriage soon began to crumble.

Although we mostly fought, there were times of reprieve and great passion. In the midst of our marital struggles, three beautiful children were born. Yet, for the most part, after they were born, Amber and I lived separate lives in the same household. My wife babysat friends' children in our home while I worked. I stayed at work as much as possible until bedtime. Then I would come home and hit the sack with our three young children nestled around me until morning. That's how our marriage worked after we had kids: Amber would do her thing, and I would do mine. We did the best we knew how at the time.

Our children, like most children would at that age, loved their mother and me unconditionally. They saw some of our fights and felt the constant tension, but they were too young to realize the implications of a failing marriage and helpless to change the situation. I cannot imagine what was going through their minds, as mine was usually numbed by medications for anxiety and depression.

After nine years of marriage, everything fell apart: Amber filed for divorce. Amber was not to blame for wanting out of the marriage; I had mood problems that were more than she could handle. She was through.

I was angry. Once again, my life was about to take another turn . . . and not for the better.

CHAPTER 2

TURNING TO THE DARK SIDE

They shouted louder and slashed themselves with
swords and spears, as was their custom, until their blood
flowed.

—1 KINGS 18:28

I met Cheri at a local pub early in the summer of 1987. Shortly
thereafter, we were sharing an apartment on Fifteenth Street
in Edmond, Oklahoma. The companionship was a welcome
relief to the stress of my nasty divorce. Busy with her MBA studies at the University of Oklahoma, Cheri was a woman in constant
motion. She'd already earned one master's degree, but her thirst
for knowledge had her striving for more. I thought we'd be great
roommates. She was attractive, intelligent, and available.

Many of those summer nights were spent poolside drinking
beer, playing sand volleyball, splashing in the pool, or unwinding
in the hot tub. This particular group of apartment dwellers was
by and large a young, hard-drinking crowd, and I was no exception. Moreover, I was making new acquaintances. In retrospect,
this socializing was the only emotional balm I had to dull the
pain of not seeing my children regularly anymore.

My college transcript showed only a few classes from ten
years back at a local university. I wondered if at thirty-one I was

too old to go back. Day after day, Cheri got off work as a professor teaching at the University of Central Oklahoma and went right back to her studies, edging closer to another master's degree. Her dedication impressed me.

On paper, Cheri and I were an educational mismatch. But in spite of my lack of formal education, we found common ground intellectually. Cheri seemed to enjoy our philosophical discussions and kept nudging me to go back to school, convinced that I could excel academically. One day, at her urging, I decided to enroll in a couple of college classes and see where it led. School made sense as a career enhancer, but just as important, it would provide a great distraction from the pain of missing my children.

I worked in sales for a nationwide chemical distributor, and this gave me the flexibility to pursue my studies by taking a few courses and still take care of my clients. With a burning desire to be the first person in my family to have a college degree, I marched down to the University of Central Oklahoma and enrolled in eighteen credit hours. I wanted to major in business and perhaps psychology.

When Cheri came home from work and saw my enrollment slip, she was a little wide-eyed but managed to say, "Wow, I am proud of you." She was probably thinking, *You have no idea how much work you just bit off,* but I'm sure she was also relieved to know that I'd be occupied with my studies and out of her hair much of the time.

✝

My first challenge came at the hands of my Birkenstock-clad, free-spirited English professor, Ms. Beck. I'd failed my first exam in grammar. I met Ms. Beck after class to discuss my test. A talented teacher and a true professional, Ms. Beck saw something in me that I hadn't seen in myself. She convinced me right away that I could do better. She also said, half-jokingly, that she thought I had Tourette's syndrome and ADHD—many who knew me would have come to the same conclusion, as my mind was in constant motion and my mouth usually followed my thoughts. She allowed me to take another exam in place of the one I had just failed, and I aced it. That was the break I needed.

I finished those eighteen hours that semester with a 4.0 GPA and was off and running. The next semester I enrolled in twenty-one hours, with the same result. Several twenty-four-hour semesters followed. After earning my undergraduate degree at the University of Central Oklahoma, I went to the University of Oklahoma for graduate work, pursuing an MBA with marketing as my major. I completed most of the hours needed for the MBA portion of the degree, but only took a few law classes and did not finish my studies due to pending legal problems. My original goal was to complete a joint MBA/JD program and then open my own business. I thought a law-based education would make me well-rounded in business; the combination of these two programs would have valuable potential.

While I excelled in school and was outwardly progressing by worldly standards, inwardly I was a mess. Still reeling from the divorce, I was hurt and lonely. The constant sense of failure, the emptiness, and my anger at a court system that told me where and when I could see my children, left me bitter and resentful.

There is an old expression that pressure doesn't build character; it reveals it. Well, I was living proof of that old maxim. Now under pressure, I was drowning in an ocean of negativity. Hopeless, afraid, and confused, I had no core beliefs and nothing on which to fix my hope.

I'd never contemplated my so-called human condition. *Why am I here? What is the meaning of life?*—all these thoughts were foreign to me. But my chronic emotional pain began to force this question upon me: *Is this pitiful, pain-addled existence all that I deserve? There has to be more.* For an ego-driven, narcissistic, secular humanist who didn't care whether he lived or died, this line of thought was dangerous.

To say I was vulnerable is an understatement. I was at a crossroads and susceptible to whichever direction the wind might blow me. Already gasping for breath, I was poised to make the queen mother of all bad decisions. As my anxiety, fear, and uncertainty began to snowball, my thought life became more erratic. My uncontrolled thoughts, my inability to bond with other people, and my "every man for himself" attitude had taken me to a lonely place. I wanted something different, something to pull me out of the emotional depths and empower me to face my trials and tribulations. Feeling weak in my soul, all I could do was search for strength—any strength.

With an undisciplined and lonely childhood, a life of disappointment, and horrible communication and relationship skills, I experienced a growing rage. My volcanic emotions stirred to the point of eruption, and a day of reckoning approached.

Cheri, now my girlfriend, was visiting her parents in Minnesota. I was alone for the next couple of weeks with nothing but time on my hands. The eighteen hours of college courses this semester weren't enough to consume my idle time or still my wandering mind. I found myself alone in that apartment, fuming at the world for my condition, angry at a God I couldn't fully believe in—at a God I *wouldn't* fully believe in—because I wouldn't allow that such a God would leave me in a state of such utter despair. God, in my mind, had abandoned me early in life. And early on, I buried Him alongside the statue of Mary in a garden in the backyard with my childhood hopes and dreams.

My sad rationale had been twisted into this thought: *If God created everything, then He created evil.* So, by that line of reasoning, I decided that God was responsible for evil, controlled it, and was in fact, both good and evil. He had to be responsible for the tragedy that was my life. And if He was responsible for all the suffering in my life, how could He possibly care about me? Since God didn't care for me, I might as well serve His enemy. If God didn't think I was good enough to save, why shouldn't I serve His evil counterpart? This evil counterpart is Satan, the god of this world. In my crippled thinking, I viewed Satan as God's alter ego.

My mind was made up. I might as well join the dark side, since that was what I had always known. Life had always been dark, even in marriage. I had always gotten into trouble, even when I thought I wanted to do good. I figured since my life had been such a mess, the God of light cared little for me. So I might as well overcome the tragedy of my life by joining the other side. At least that way I could be more up front about my own darkness. I didn't have to be hypocritical anymore. I was intent on making changes . . . no matter what.

✝✚

One Saturday afternoon, as I sat on my red corduroy couch, my heart filled with anger toward a God who seemed distant, even cruel. My tiny snatches of knowledge about this God of the Bible had built the picture of a tyrant in my mind's eye: a God who is never satisfied, just waiting for one of His followers to step out of line. In my thinking, God was secretly hoping one of His followers would sin or fail so He could make an example to His other followers and make them stay in line. I felt that the moral world of man was such that the deck was stacked against him, that man could never measure up. Hadn't God created a fear-based system with the threat of hell that forced people to bend their knees to Him, not out of love, but out of self-preservation? What did free will mean in all this? I was consumed by my tortured thoughts.

Finally, I said, "God, I will not serve You. I will not serve a God of fear and punishment, who forces His victims into submission. I will serve the dark side." And I blurted, "Satan, come into my life. You are now my god. Use me, have me, and control me for your purposes." Having finally made *some* kind of spiritual decision, I felt a little relief.

Immediately, a power swept over me. A stark emptiness filled my inner core. Vile and perverted thoughts invaded my mind. My spirit felt dark. To my immediate right, the couch cushion sank as if someone had sat down next to me. A voice came to me and said, *"Go to the bookstore."* I went to a large chain bookstore, not knowing what I would do when I got there. I walked through the aisles, and somehow my hands found the satanic bible and the *Book of Shadows.*

The cashier looked nervous as I approached with my books. After hesitating for a moment, she spoke to me. "You don't have to buy these books. You have a choice."

Her boldness made me hesitate, but I bought the books anyway. I sensed in my spirit that she was praying for me. I left the store and never looked back.

As I walked up the flight of stairs to the apartment, my heart was heavy and burdened. As I opened the door, a cool rush of air surrounded me. With my book purchases in one hand, I closed the door behind me. In my spirit, I knew what was about to take place was wrong; I knew I was in a dangerous place; I was in a state of defiant rebellion; I was headed to a place of no return.

I ignored the pang of my conscience that had given me pause. I sat on the couch and opened the satanic bible. Something terrible happened in my spirit just then. When I opened that dark book, I sensed that heavenly angels were commanded by God to let go due to my conscious choice to serve the bad side. From my earliest memories, I believed in angels and spiritual beings. I am not certain why; I just did. What I didn't realize was that there were some of these beings seemingly watching over me with protective custody, perhaps as an older brother would his little sister, or a lioness would her cubs.

As I began to read the satanic bible, I sensed a dark presence sweep over my body. I left the book open on the couch and got up to turn on the stereo. I put a CD in and returned to reading. The more I read, the more the room filled with the presence of dark and powerful beings. While a wave of nausea swept over me, I was exhilarated at the same time. My heavy heart turned cold all at once, and it felt as if there were a protective wall that surrounded me—an aura of evil designed to fend off opposing doctrine and thought. A dense and dark covering enveloped me, claiming me as its own.

The warmth and light of the sun faded outside the apartment

just as any remnant of light faded from my life. The air chilled as I turned the pages in these wicked books, their pernicious thoughts invading my heart and twisting my soul. Hours passed, and like a small boat set adrift on the open sea, I was about to be thrust headlong into a violent storm.

The enemy moved in quickly, capturing my thoughts; he had found a malleable subject. I was informed that a sacrifice needed to be paid to show my allegiance; it would repeal the opposition from the saints.

Moments later, the skin on my left forearm sank and then parted as a sharp paring knife entered my body for the first time. The wooden handle became sticky as it absorbed the blood that spewed outward. There was neither pain nor regret as the blood covenant was made. At this very moment, the threshold had been crossed; any semblance of virtue, innocence, or purity was gone.

I do not remember the rest of the night, but when I woke up the next morning, my left arm had a deep gash in it. Blood spotted the bedsheets and carpet that led to the couch in the living room. My right hand held a knife. I threw the knife on the floor as I got out of bed and went into the kitchen to make coffee. I didn't question my surroundings or really remember or care about what happened the night before. I had to go to school, put in a few hours at work, and continue my typical day.

I wasn't alone anymore, as I had always felt. It was obvious and very real to me that my mind and body seemed to house "company." I knew my body well; I smelled, tasted, and breathed differently than I had just hours ago. My spirit had changed. I now felt as if I weighed more physically. It was as if alien beings had climbed inside of me and were "setting up house." Part of me sensed I was in deep, deep trouble. Another part of me was ready for the new adventure that lay ahead of me.

Each day that passed after I committed to the devil, I felt more directed and focused. I continued with my classes, but other areas of my life suffered. I had no real friends at the time and began to seclude myself even more from the outside world. Isolated and withdrawn, I was losing touch with my emotions, while at the same time, I was experiencing a heightened awareness in my spirit.

Now ensconced in Satan's spiritual incubator, my senses became more acute and refined. As my emotions and feelings started to fade, my sense of smell, sight, and hearing became enhanced and well developed. Like an animal's, my baser instincts became the focus while my spirit was going through a complete makeover to equip me to do my master's bidding. I was being spiritually redirected for Satan's purposes. And as I would soon see, sins of the flesh are his stock in trade.

I felt more directed in life now, a man with a new mission. I wasn't throwing caution to the wind as much since there were new desires in my heart. New, instinctive motives were working in me. During one of my nights of drinking and soaking in the community hot tub, I met a woman who lived in the building adjacent to mine. She was a recent divorcée with a couple of children who visited on weekends.

Sandra was an artist, tall and attractive. One day she came over to ask if I could help her with her car, which wouldn't start. I jump-started her car, and as the car was warming up, she asked me into her apartment for a cup of coffee. Within twenty minutes, we were in bed. About once a week thereafter, she would call me and tell me her car was having problems. I would go over each time with the same results. Despite my relationship with Cheri, my regular visits to Sandra went on for nearly a year before she moved.

After a simple look around our world, it's easy to surmise that much of Satan's deception is built on sex, lust, and pleasures of the flesh. It was no accident that wherever I went, women seemed to be mystically drawn to me. Satan's goal was to use my now white-hot appetite for sex to lure women into relationships that would be anything but fun and games.

So I was dispatched by my newfound spiritual master to sexually prey upon weak women, and the women he sent me usually claimed to be Christians. His mission in me was to take a lukewarm Christian woman and put her far from God's will, to take her off course. I would lure her into sin, ultimately separating her from the One she professed to follow.

A typical assignment looked like this: I'd get involved in a singles group in a local church. Most of these women were not particularly discerning, and nearly all were looking for a relationship. In this vulnerable state, many were an easy mark for someone willing to say or do anything to get what he wanted.

Some of the women I encountered over the next ten years were admittedly from the dark side. Two humans supercharged by satanic lust are all about self-gratification. Satanism is essentially all about self; it literally forces you to turn inward in such a way that all of your thoughts are dominated by the desire to please the self. It makes you a slave to every lustful, selfish notion that the flesh can invent. It's about as close to hell on earth as you can get. Although the flesh is reaping sensual pleasure and satisfaction, the spirit is dying a slow and possibly permanent death.

I was finding out that the flesh has few limits in terms of its desires, and my thrill seeking didn't end with sexual encounters.

✝

I played racquetball regularly at my complex. I loved the action, the pace of the game, and the one-on-one competition. I had a friend, an Oklahoma State graduate, who worked for a pharmaceutical vendor I called on. We'd hit the courts weekly when he was in town, and the games were intense. But in this insatiable mode I was falling into, I wanted more.

So I devised a way to make racquetball more exciting, exhilarating, and of course more dangerous. I put a radio in the rear of the gym and cranked up the volume to create more distraction, forcing us to concentrate harder. However, the next touch really showed the state of my decline: we'd both smoke pot before the match so our senses would be dulled, increasing our chances of being hit by a ball moving at high speeds, crashing into a wall, or even running into each other. In the history of stupid ideas, "marijuana racquetball" stacks up to most anything I've ever heard. I know what you're thinking here; you think I am proud of these shenanigans. But let me tell you, it's not with any pride that I retell this story. It's just one of the many steps that marked my downward spiral.

✝

I practiced my new religion in secret, at night, alone in the apartment when Cheri was traveling. The ceremonies seem so cliché now: a candlelit room and music by the Doors or something eerily similar at a high volume. I ushered in demonic assistance and had the usual blood sacrifice. Like a drunk the morning after his bender, I wouldn't remember the previous night's activities until I noticed the candles, the robe, the knife, or the satanic bible lying open. Similar to perhaps a nervous teenager hiding his beer cans and bong, I would dispose of my satanic paraphernalia and go about my regular day.

This lifestyle was something akin to being in a spiritual trance . . . I was literally taken over, detached from the moment. The emotional and physical baggage of these nocturnal experiences began to weigh on me. I lived in a state of constant heaviness and fatigue. I was drifting far away from any modicum of joy and peace I'd known and into a place of emotional chaos. Satan lured me in, and I not only had taken the bait but was swallowing the hook.

I studied the dark arts with the same laser focus that had given me a 4.0 GPA in my college work. I was drawn more and more to the immediate gratification that this lifestyle was bringing. It's a strange dichotomy: I was willing to trade the constant depression for the self-gratification and the "power surges" this life brought to me. The nightly exhilaration of practicing this wicked craft became like a drug, and I was becoming like an addict—more and more of the drug was required to achieve the same thrill. The enemy was sharpening my appetites. I was a gluttonous animal being led to slaughter.

Satanism is practiced in various ways, and doctrine varies according to the believer or group of believers. One of the most popular forms is LaVeyan satanism, named after Anton Szandor LaVey. He founded the Church of Satan in 1966. He also authored the satanic bible in 1969. Most other forms are considered theistic satanism and share various beliefs, ceremonies, and rituals. For the most part, theistic satanism involves a worship of a single deity, namely Satan. In LaVeyan satanism, Satan is used more as a symbol of carnality and earthly values. LaVeyan satanists believe this is man's inherent nature, and we are to submit to those natural desires and tendencies.

The LaVeyan satanic religion is so much about self that the most celebrated holiday of the year is the believer's own birthday, a day highly cherished in a satanist's life. The second most celebrated holiday of the year would be Walpurgis Night (or the "witches' Sabbath"), in honor of Saint Walpurga. The third most celebrated holiday for the LaVeyan satanist (and ironically number two for Christians) is Halloween. Once I had committed my life to Satan, Halloween became a special night for me. I would typically spend it alone and practice some form of a solitary ritual that was more directed perhaps—meaning that it seemed more concentrated and spiritually driven.

Halloween in the United States is recognized widely, and if it isn't the most celebrated holiday, it is a close second to Christmas. To me, it shows how invasive Satan has become in the American lifestyle. After all, it's not like we are celebrating the coming of All Saints' Day; we are indulging baser instincts and playing with our darker sides. Halloween is centered on the dead, ghosts, ghouls, spirits, and macabre. People mask themselves with costumes and portray themselves as something they are not. Children go trick-or-treating. This involves going to neighborhood houses and asking for candy and treats. The faster they go from house to house, the more they get. For many people, Halloween is all about self-indulgence and greed, the gratification of the flesh. I believe that this is one of the many ways that Satan slips into our culture unnoticed.

In my personal experiences with satanism, I incorporated a mix of LaVeyan satanism and theistic satanism. I do not claim to be an expert on either. I did my own style of satanic practice. I simply served Satan the only way I knew to: guided through prayer. I read the satanic bible and other writings. I did my own ritual practices to derive power, and I prayed.

I didn't look like a satanist and wasn't part of any organized coven, or group of satanists. I didn't feel the need to get involved with anyone else to pursue my new desires. In fact, I thought that group practice was a weakness, despite the claims that satanism brought more power in a group setting.

Again, I in no way claim to be an expert on satanism or the many other dark religions. I can only attest to my experiences on the dark side and how those choices nearly took my life.

The pain of my divorce was a still-daily battle. I was angry, hurt, and resentful, and I wanted to get even. And if I hadn't been absorbed with school by day and the dark arts at night, I may have tried to retaliate. It is a strange paradox that might have been a bad country song: "If I hadn't been too busy with satanism, I mighta killed my ex."

My children came to the apartment every other weekend

for visitation, and we enjoyed activities together. They were very young at the time, and it was easy for me to sneak my actions around them. I loved my kids very much, but I was so tied up in my own little world I didn't think about how the consequences of my actions could affect them in the future.

My daughter Kristin was about six years old. One day she told me she wasn't coming over any longer. When I asked her why, she said, "Dad, God knows what you are doing and doesn't like it." She stayed away for months but returned from time to time because of her love for me. I knew she had a spiritual gift of discernment. I had that gift along with words of knowledge that I would get about various people in my life. Whatever gifts God had given me, Satan was twisting. Instead of a gift from God used to help His people and expand His kingdom, it became a weapon to deceive, manipulate, and destroy.

✝

Within a few months of my pact with Satan, during a ritual I was having, I began inviting demons into my life. Most came from regions in England, Scotland, and Ireland. I know you're wondering, how did I know where they came from? Did the Scottish demon have an unintelligible accent? Did the Irish demon want to fight the other two? Did perhaps the English demon show up and say, "Mike, be a good chap and put on that bloody awful Morrison fellow, turn up the volume, and let's get on with this self-mutilation. I do have a schedule to keep"?

Not quite. The horrifying truth is that I was given names to call on, specific demons to invite into my life (names I will not disclose now), often through the ritual of blood sacrifice.

This may have involved cutting myself or animal sacrifice. On this particular night, the power was overwhelming. Something unique was happening, as though something or someone significant was present but I couldn't nail it down. With music by the Doors blaring, I was channeling through my spirit guide and could sense something was changing as I felt a crushing burden.

The next day I learned that a double homicide had occurred about three blocks from my apartment. A man who worked at a local veterans' hospital went to his girlfriend's house and murdered both her and her baby girl. Both baby and mother had pentagrams carved in their stomachs. It was very clear to authorities that this was not only satanic in nature but some form of ritualistic killing.

The man was found guilty in a court of law and was sentenced to death. A few years later, he was executed. After hearing about the murders, I carried on that day with feelings that ranged between disgust and enlightenment. I was filled with thoughts of having gained some sense of power from what had happened. I felt connected to the murders and seemed to have graduated in the spirit and reached a new level of power and control. It was as though I had been present in the room, and possibly was, in the spirit. I felt very heavy. I thought about how the two died and the pain they suffered. I thought about their unheard cries for help. I thought about the mother's pleas to a God who allowed such a torturous death. Once again, the evil prevailed in this battle between life and death. I felt a spiritual union with the murderer, who was obviously directed by the powerful new god I served.

The forces of darkness were granting me favor, and it intrigued me. My confidence soared with a new sense of security that the one I now served would take care of me, guide me, and offer me protection. I couldn't have been more deceived.

✝

As I raced through my undergrad studies at UCO, I got acquainted with a guy in a psych class who would ultimately become a friend.

Mitch Perkins seemed very intelligent and was working toward a business major. He would later earn his MBA. I found Mitch interesting, a deep thinker, and someone I connected with on an intellectual level. I found myself spending more and more time with Mitch as we moved through the semester. Looking back, I know now that my interest in him was purely due to his knowledge and the possible ways I could use it to further manipulate and control others. Mitch seemed to be a bright guy with a vast understanding of religion and philosophy. I loved both subjects; both had been studied for thousands of years and appealed to my inquiring mind.

Our discussions varied, but they would inevitably end up with his speaking about his faith, how he loved God, and his belief in Jesus Christ. Mitch sensed I was troubled. He sensed my disturbance and perhaps mental imbalance. I had to be a strange sight to him. He saw me buzzing through school, having relationships, employed, yet troubled to the point that I could have been diagnosed with multiple mental illnesses. His obvious faith in Christ didn't threaten me. I just thought I would let him play his games, learn from him, and move on. I was spiritually arrogant. I thought I could toy with believers because of my "superior" spiritual knowledge and my increasing powers from the dark side.

Out of kindness, Mitch began to seek me out to just be around me and later told me he prayed for me constantly. I didn't want him at my house and tried to dissuade him from coming by. He would come anyway, especially when I was in class. I could tell because I would get home and notice crosses above my door made with holy oil. They seemed to glow after dark. Maybe he used some kind of reflective oil; I am not sure, but I always saw the crosses.

Mitch had a prayer group that was in intense prayer for me at this time. Bill Fernandez, Sonnae Albert, and many others stayed faithfully in prayer for me to receive Christ. Sonnae is a prayer warrior; she is about eighty-eight years old now and is still strong in the Lord and in her intercessory prayers for others. She is a remarkable lady with deep knowledge of the Word of God. When I initially met her, she told me that someday I would be saved, that I would be a warrior for God, spread the gospel, teach ministers, and speak to the nations. Inwardly, I laughed.

Although I had moments of clarity of mind and moments of temporary happiness throughout this stage in my life, most often I was burdened with negative and depressing thoughts. I continued to try to reason my way out of these thoughts using the philosophy and logic I had learned in college. Yet, my mind propelled me into a vast, outer darkness. The more I tried to discern where I was and where I was going, and the more I tried to think through my thoughts and my circumstances, the more I became intertwined with a complex and ever-increasing vortex of possibilities, doctrines, and philosophies. It was a crazy process: the more I tried to reason, the more unreasonable things got.

After a year of dating, my relationship with Cheri began to fall apart. A few times she told me she sensed that something had changed. She didn't know what, but I wasn't the same. Once, when we were together intimately, she told me that I scared her. Our relationship felt strange, she said, as if she were with someone else. When she closed her eyes, she felt as if a car were on top of her and she couldn't breathe. She was being smothered. She commented that she felt as if she had just slept with many men. I believe she was actually sleeping with many; they just weren't men. I was demon-possessed.

After several instances like this, we stopped sleeping together and drifted apart. She started going home more and more to see her parents. I later found out she was having relations with another man she went to high school with. I was offended by her secrecy even though I was also having affairs, but my mind was elsewhere.

In looking back, while I was living in the apartment with Cheri, I was restricted in how deep I could go in my solitary rituals and practices. With her coming and going, not to mention the nearly round-the-clock activity of an apartment community, I knew my satanic practices could draw unwanted attention. I wanted more privacy. The enemy wanted me isolated and alone.

Cheri grew unhappy with our living arrangement. Her statements were telling: "I don't think our place is cozy anymore," and "I feel a deep sense of dread every time I'm coming home." So she stayed away with her friends or studied in the university library.

I looked for a new place and found a condo located nearby. I leased a truck and moved my belongings in one afternoon. When

Cheri came home, I told her I was out. In our final conversation, she told me she felt confusion and chaos around both me and the apartment.

My spiritual condition was palpable to those around me, and it was about to get worse . . . much worse. I handed her the keys and left.

CHAPTER 3

SUBMISSION TO EVIL

This is the verdict: Light has come into the world, but
people loved darkness instead of light because their
deeds were evil. Everyone who does evil hates the light,
and will not come into the light for fear that their deeds
will be exposed.

—JOHN 3:19–20

I t was early August 1990 when I moved into the condo on Abilene Street. My time was marked by my utter preoccupation with anything spiritual. I found the darkness so alluring. While I maintained normalcy at both work and school, everything took a backseat to my submission to evil. In and out of court almost weekly for child support hearings, I watched my financial situation begin to unravel.

Making ends meet became a daily struggle. My nocturnal activities were hindering my sales, and my paychecks suffered. I used money from student loans not just for books and tuition but for rent, groceries, and gas. Pink slips eventually came from several companies when my sales diminished, and I could always count on the court sending garnishment papers. At this time, I worked for several chemical distributors and manufacturers; each job ended when I could not keep up with sales goals. I was plunging headlong into emotional, spiritual, relational, and financial brokenness. Satan was pulling me ever downward into depression and hopelessness, and I saw no way out.

But the move to Abilene Street gave me something I'd been craving: the privacy to carry on my nighttime activities unnoticed; or at least that's what I thought. What I didn't count on was that most of my new neighbors on this suburban, middle-class street turned out to be Christians. In Oklahoma, what many would call part of the Bible Belt, it is common to talk about one's faith and church. Within a few weeks of settling in, the neighbors were on me like bees on honey. Abilene Street was a short one with few adjoining condos, and everyone knew each other. The neighbors gathered regularly for cookouts and ice cream socials.

They shared life stories, kid stories, and humorous stories of their families. These stories made me reflect on how disjointed and dysfunctional my biological family was; we had few times like these families were sharing. It also brought to mind my separation from my own children. I only got to see them four days a month, and that was not acceptable to me. The neighbors also shared stories of God and church. I wondered why they gushed so much about their faith. I could not gush about mine.

I avoided these settings as much as possible. But I lived on the last house on the cul-de-sac, so they seemed to gather in my front yard.

Had I known that this small neighborhood was so close-knit, I wouldn't have moved in. I seldom ventured outside unless it was to meet one of the single ladies on the block or to get my mail. My garage was in the back alley, so it was convenient for coming and going unnoticed.

There were many instances of neighbors knocking on my door just to say hello or to bring me a home-cooked meal. Yet, I could detect their hidden motives: what they really wanted was to know my business. They were friendly but too transparent. I wanted privacy, and they wanted community. They asked me a lot of questions: Was I single? How many kids did I have? What church did I go to? All normal stuff, I suppose, but I wasn't there to socialize or to share my experiences—especially not the dark path I had chosen.

Their children gathered in the street in the cul-de-sac by my house. They played basketball at the neighborhood court that was adjacent to my house. They had picnics in the community gazebo. I would hear them daily. My memories went to my childhood and how sad I always was. Their laughter mesmerized me. I thought of how innocent and naive these children were to the pain and evil I had experienced. They enjoyed laughing and being free to express themselves. Their happy noises always took me back in time to when I was a child and made me remember how I felt trapped in a young person's body with no way out.

While they were having fun, I was becoming addicted to an isolated existence: locked doors, drawn shades, solitude. I only had my children every other weekend, and the times I was alone without them became increasingly unhealthy both spiritually and mentally. This period gave me time to sink lower, get angrier, and continue to pursue dark spiritual interests.

✝

Tracy Yates and his wife, both of whom were Christians, lived right next door. They sensed I was struggling and let me know I was in their prayers. Our houses were joined by a common wall ten inches thick. Each side of the street had condo homes that were joined with a single firewall separating them. I was living alone, but my condo was close enough to my new neighbors that anything out of the ordinary could be detected. And of course, it didn't take long for this to happen.

One night I was stressed and felt weak. I drew strength from my ritual time (RT, I called it), when I performed my satanic practices alone, in the dark of night. The rituals were fairly similar but grew darker and more intense. Typically, I would light candles, pray to Satan, and wait for things to happen. There was nearly always blood spilled. It was usually mine, but at times it was a neighborhood animal, usually a cat. I hated cats because of the memories they stirred up. Cats seemed evil to me. I remember having cat scratch fever as a child and being very ill for two weeks. Cats also symbolized arrogant independence to me, much like most of the women I had known throughout my life. Although my heart was being hardened through these cruel animal rituals, there was still something inside convicting me of the wrong in it. A war between good and evil lived in me.

The isolation of these practices was addictive and drew me into deeper depression. I was losing control in my life, but the one time I thought I had control occurred during these dark nights. It seems ironic, but this was my time, my space, and my will. I was so wrong. This was Satan's time in my life, and he was ruling it.

As with any rule or tradition, exceptions surfaced. Nighttime rituals would occasionally need to be moved to daylight hours, especially when the pressures of the world closed in on me. After one of these, on a cool fall day, I stumbled outside in a daze, and Tracy spotted me with blood dripping down my arm, my eyes fixed in a wild stare. Tracy was surprised and concerned. Whatever garbled excuse I came up with for my condition, I'm sure he wasn't buying it. But being the man he was, he helped me clean up and apply bandages to my arm.

In my spiritually defiled state, it was easy for me to sense his innocence and the holy covering that enveloped him. I prayed against him, asking for protection from the prayers I knew he had begun to utter on my behalf. I became more agitated and uneasy around him and made efforts to avoid him. The darkness within me hated any form of light, and this Christian man was bathed in it. In my darkened world, this made him my enemy.

✝

On the opposite side of Tracy lived a strikingly beautiful young woman named Karen. Vivacious, caring, and good-hearted, she often spent evenings with me, sipping beer out in the warm nighttime air while we carried on deep, philosophical conversations. Karen was also the owner of a gorgeous, long-haired black cat that I'd become intrigued with. Despite my aversion to cats, I had a bizarre connection with that animal, as if it could see right through me. Sensing my need for companionship, Karen graciously offered to give me Sanibel. She said she felt I needed the company more than she did.

Sanibel was in my care for only a couple weeks when I was directed to kill her in a sacrifice. One evening, I smothered the breath from the animal and then breathed life back into her until she came to. I did this five to six times until I decided to let her go. She breathed her last breath with her green eyes focused on mine. The sense of power this gave me was euphoric. The ability to snatch life from something innocent was an aphrodisiac-like rush that fed my growing addiction. Breathing life back into her gave me an equal rush. I cycled between the two experiences—really just the one experience of controlling life—until I got tired. She was the first of many animal killings in that house.

Later that night, I took Sanibel's lifeless body, wrapped it in a black trash bag, and threw it in a city Dumpster. The darkness within me was growing.

†

Across the street from Karen lived a widow about the same age. Her husband was in the armed forces and died in an accident in a training mission. Jennifer and her young son, Travis, lived alone. They sometimes came down to my house to visit. We would spend time together drinking and carrying on about the usual: school, life, and romance.

Jennifer occasionally had a free weekend when the grandparents came to get Travis for a visit. One Friday evening when her in-laws picked up Travis early, she came down by herself, and we sat on my patio for our normal conversation and had about ten beers between us. When it cooled down outside, she came in my house to a warm fireplace to continue our conversation. Shortly after that, we were all over each other on the couch until we moved to the bedroom. These dalliances continued off and on over the next ten months until she eventually moved.

Next door to Jennifer lived a model. Angela also had a dual career in the publishing business and was very friendly, outgoing, and bubbly. She had a fiancé and seemed quite happy. We spoke often as I walked past her house on my way to Henry Hudson's, a local watering hole. We became friends, sharing cocktails together when her fiancé was out of town and talking, laughing, and flirting a little. Then one evening after a few drinks, we ended up in bed.

These examples are not for me to convince you that I was a talented lothario. It's to show that the flesh is an enormous part of satanism. It is all about immediate self-gratification. It's ultimately about making people slaves to their own desires. In my growing state of becoming more and more isolated and withdrawn, I was still active in my pursuit of the weak and prideful.

This satanic thought pattern leads to the kind of predatory sex that harms women, destroys marriages, and robs virtue from the innocent. It is, by its nature, destructive. My secret, demonic agenda was to engage as many young, innocent women as I could. There were days on that street when three or four encounters were commonplace. Sex was a game; women were objects. I was trapped in a state of perpetual craving with ultimately no satisfaction. With one conquest finished, I was on to the next.

✝

Tim and Desiree Good, young newlyweds and born-again believers, lived across the street from me. Desiree was a lovely girl with a wonderful spirit. Tim seemed equally good-hearted and upright. They were a strong couple. Occasionally my spirit would receive an assignment against them, but it would always be shut down. My heart was drawn to them, and I know Satan hated this. It's clear to me now that God had a huge hedge of protection around them. Many times my thoughts drifted to Desiree.

I know these thoughts were meant for harm, but the power that surrounded them kept me at bay.

Former NFL player Ron Watkins and his wife were neighbors as well. Ron was very active in a church not far from where I lived at that time, so much so that he eventually became the head pastor there.

On the other side of Ron lived a young couple who were also devout Christians. Dennis and Michelle lived out their faith with genuine kindness to me and my children. They walked the walk. But they were not just good; they were also wise. It wasn't long before Michelle became very uneasy around me, sensing that all was not right with me. She felt the evil that surrounded me, and I believe God led her to separate herself and her family from me for their own protection.

✝

The rage I felt toward Amber, my ex-wife, was hard to suppress. This had been a growing feeling in me, created long before she asked me to leave her house and had divorce papers served. And it didn't help my disposition one bit that she'd acquired a new boyfriend who I felt was both condescending and sarcastic toward me. I was divorced, unemployed, and brokenhearted, and now I thought my ex-wife's boyfriend, Chuck, was making fun of me in front of my children. Chuck could bring out the worst in me. He made my blood boil.

So imagine my joy when Chuck and my ex-wife purchased a home less than a mile from me. Chuck was an avid jogger, and I began to notice him coming by my house at the same time every day. This was no accident; I'm certain he did this to taunt me. (If Chuck had known the depth of my emotional and spiritual problems, I'm sure he could have bought a house in Japan and it wouldn't have been far enough away from his new wife's insane ex.)

As Chuck took his daily runs by my house, I began to think about retaliation. I thought long and hard about just running out of my house and attacking him. But I knew that would be too obvious and would lead to more legal troubles. So I hatched a plan.

Chuck jogged in a part of town that was somewhat deserted, with a large field next to the road where he ran. A wooden stockade fence bordered the property for much of the path and abruptly ended at one end. I could hide behind the fence, armed with a baseball bat, and club him as he jogged by. No one would ever see it. I'd attack him under the cover of darkness and then sneak away undetected. Who could convict me? Even if I was suspected, I was sure that nobody could ever prove anything. I felt confident I could create an alibi and get away with Operation Kill Chuck.

So, decked out in dark clothing, I drove to the jogging path late one evening. I parked my car nearby, slipped on a black ski mask, and hid behind the fence. Within minutes, I heard footsteps as I saw Chuck running toward me. I felt my heart beating faster as my hands gripped the wooden bat. My disdain for Chuck mounted as I saw him coming closer. I wanted to kill him, to take his life that very moment. With my heart beating in my head, I held my breath and waited. As he came fully into view, I noticed him wearing earphones, listening to music. *He's twenty feet away . . . now ten.* My thoughts were focused, intent. *Almost, almost . . .* Then suddenly I sprang from my hiding spot and swung with all the evil rage that churned inside me.

But I'd miscalculated my attack. Chuck was already several paces ahead, so when I swung I missed him completely. The momentum of the swing without hitting my target caused me to stumble and nearly fall. I stood there in the night air, staring at the bat, wondering how that had just happened. Chuck's blood was not on the bat; his body was not shaking uncontrollably on the pavement, like in the vision I had prior to this episode. Chuck neither saw nor heard me. With his headphones blaring, he jogged off into the warm night air.

After my first bizarre near hit with Chuck, I revisited my hiding place several times with the same intention. I would sit behind the fence and wait for him to approach. As he drew near, I would ready myself with bat in hand and then just watch him jog by. In some strange way, I began to pity him. He seemed just as miserable as I was, if not more so. Previously, before I saw the real Chuck, I thought he was content and happy. But from observing his attitude and actions, I realized how unhappy and dejected he was. It seemed that killing him would only put him out of his misery. And the way I saw it, such a man deserved to live on in suffering. His relationship with Amber couldn't last. She wouldn't put up with what I thought to be his mistreatment and his junk forever. I would punish him more by letting him live.

As I began to count the costs, the idea of ending up in jail or losing access to my children began to quell any deep desire for revenge. My hideouts also provided some moments for honest reflection. While waiting in the woods for Chuck, I was struck by the reality that something inside of me wasn't quite right, not that this insight changed me one little bit. I was determined to rebel against all who hurt me and especially against any kind of authority figure in my life.

✝

During this period, I met a guy named Brian Sanders through a friend of mine at school. A few years younger than I was, Brian was a professed Christian and was yet another man who sensed the darkness I was in and would try to speak to me of Jesus. Within a few months of meeting me, he introduced me to his father, Dr. Robert Sanders. Bob was a psychologist and a strong Christian who took an interest in my life and in my "story," as he called it.

Bob and I would meet occasionally at a coffee shop or local hamburger joint and discuss our religions and belief systems, and we would share time together. For some reason I never felt threatened by Bob and actually enjoyed his company even though he was on the other side of the fence from me, spiritually speaking. He was nonthreatening and didn't try to shove his theology down my throat. He was okay by me.

✝

On the night of November 26, 1992, I played with my three children in front of a warm fireplace at my condo. We played Yahtzee and cards. We drank hot cocoa and worked on a school arts and crafts project for one of the children. At the time, Marisa was twelve; Kristin, ten; and Jason, eight. In the middle of this lighthearted time, I was suddenly covered with feelings of despair. I thought, *Why would the spirits be bothering me right now? This is my time.* Almost immediately my doorbell rang and my brother Dennis was at the door with the answer. With tears pooling in his eyes, he stood on the porch, looking like a broken-hearted child, and said, "Dad just died."

I stared at him with vacant, soulless eyes. Without a trace of emotion, I replied, "Thank you for letting me know."

Dennis tried to embrace me, but I closed the door. I went back inside and started playing with my children. They asked me who it was.

"Oh, that was Uncle Dennis. He came by to tell me my dad died."

The kids stopped playing and sat there staring at my lack of emotions. Though they were not close to my mom or dad, they were unsettled that their granddad had just died and their dad was emotionless. Even children sense such incongruity. My children, particularly my eldest, Marisa, looked at me as if I were an alien. I can imagine their thoughts: *Why isn't he crying or upset? What's wrong with Dad?*

We continued playing and didn't discuss my father's death. Really, I loved my father more than any other member of my family. But Satan had turned my heart to stone to the point that tears weren't even possible. The cracks that Satan had made in my soul were starting to fissure, and my emotional lifeblood was seeping out. I was being pulled into a dark and desperate, emotionless void, with my heart and soul dying for lack of light.

✝

Dad's funeral came and went. I attended with the rest of my family but didn't interact a lot. Since I wasn't close to my family, I had little to say. I don't remember the funeral in general, as I had taken three or four pain pills prior to the service. What I do remember is how shallow my family life was at the time.

The funeral made me reflect for a moment on my dark activities. In my mind, I fast-forwarded to my own death. I pictured my body in the casket, with no one at the service, not even a priest. I only saw black vultures hovering above an empty church in a vacant land.

I had a moment of sorrow about a week after my father's death when I went to his grave site and sliced open my arm with a sharpened knife, blood spilling out at his grave site from the veins of his lost and broken son. I didn't shed a tear as the blood rolled down my arm. A cemetery employee witnessed my private ceremony, saw my bloodstained arm, and called authorities. Paramedics and police showed up minutes later.

In a strange twist, one of the police officers who arrived on the scene happened to be a friend who ministered to me for an hour or so until he realized I was carrying a gun. He coaxed the gun out of my hand, and in an act of kindness, he followed me home and didn't press any charges.

†

I didn't leave my house for a solid month. My anger and depression reached new lows.

One day during that month, I sat on my bed, the Doors blaring, holding a small .25 caliber revolver with a single bullet in the chamber. As the music and a great wave of my own depression reached their crest, I put the revolver to my right temple and pulled the trigger. *Click*. I spun the revolver again and pulled the trigger. *Click*. This went on for at least an hour. I finally stopped, pointed the gun at the ceiling, pulled the trigger, and pierced the ceiling with a small hole.

I grew more desperate by the day. I'd burned through all my personal savings and spent all my student loan money. I was divorced, friendless, and alone. Behind on my rent, I was soon evicted. All these pressures and stressors thrust me into searching for something I was good at in my life. The only thing I felt connected with at the time was my religion, so I continued to practice satanism, which seemed to give me a sense of control in the uncontrollable world that surrounded me.

I held on to my depression, hate, and anger with a viselike ferocity. This was the fruit of my satanic harvest, and I refused to surrender it. I was intent on holding on to the dark power I'd gained. So I set my heart like granite and refused the love that my godly neighbors tried to shower on me. But I soon realized that stopping the spread of light, even into a darkened soul, could be a difficult task, and their kind acts lit a small candle in the dark cavern of my soul.

I was a drowning man being pulled under by a riptide of deceit. My sweet neighbors threw me a rope to help pull me from the dark pit I was in. But being hard-hearted, I wouldn't allow myself to be vulnerable, to offer anyone access into the wreckage that my life had become. I refused to grab hold of the lifeline that could have saved me. Instead, I chose to wallow in the evil mire that had become me.

CHAPTER 4

TRAINED TO DECEIVE

But everything exposed by the light becomes visible—and everything that is illuminated becomes a light. This is why it is said: "Wake up, sleeper, rise from the dead, and Christ will shine on you."

—EPHESIANS 5:13–14

After about two years of living at the house on Abilene, I moved to a new location in Edmond. A commission check I had been awaiting from the last company I worked for enabled me to put a deposit and first month's rent down on a house on Apollo Road. This neighborhood was different from the last; this was a party block, and it fed perfectly into my lifestyle. I was the only single man on my street, and on the weekends the married guys wanted to come over, drink beer, and flirt with my lady friends.

Maintaining a relationship with my children during this period of my life was challenging. Although they visited every other weekend, I was limited financially and couldn't take them out to eat or enjoy other entertainment, so we hung around the house, played games, rode bikes, and worked on their schoolwork. When at my house, the children jumped in my bed at night, crawled around me, and went to sleep. They had repeated this behavior since they were toddlers. They were also fearful of the houses I lived in. I have been in a lot of haunted houses in my life, but most of these were the ones I lived in. Very strange things happened in this house: lights and TVs going on and off by themselves, material items moving on their own, snakes in the house, as well as thousands of spiders at once, and continual strange noises at all times of night. The kids and their friends were often frightened.

When the kids came over, I taught them how to hide from the guy trying to repossess my car. This man knew where I lived and tried for eight months to confiscate it. We also tried to dodge people trying to serve me with legal papers for court proceedings related to divorce issues. I would have the kids go outside and scope out surrounding directions, cars, and sidewalks to see if a possible unfriendly person was around. They got pretty good at these covert missions and became aware of who was a potential enemy. When I was home alone, I parked my car on a different street and jumped the back fence to avoid detection or confrontation.

I knew I was coming to the end of an era. I believed that somehow I would be free from all the hiding and all the running. I sensed I would soon be separated from my kids but almost felt relief in that. I wasn't stable and started to realize my judgment or my ability to rationalize was in someone else's power. I was fading quickly into another realm of existence. I visited the spirit world often and felt that at any moment I would be unable to return to the natural world I lived in. The trapdoor that separated two parallel existences would close, and I would be lost forever to an eternity in an unknown dimension.

Socially, things were improving, but a black cloud of darkness continued to stalk until it affected every area of my life. Spiritual bankruptcy was a reality for me. But it was worse than that. Some people say, "Well, things can't get much worse," but that's not true. Believe me: things can always get worse on this earth. There seemed to be no light at the end of the tunnel. Hopelessness was constant. My thoughts went from dark to darker, resulting in actions becoming darker.

I had a more concentrated life of prayer to Satan. There was more arm and body cutting. When I practiced self-mutilation for spiritual reasons, to show my obedience and therefore gain a deeper sense of power from my loyalty to Satan, the cuts on my body became deeper and inflicted greater injury.

Dark spiritual influence on my external actions was growing. My carnal thoughts became more extreme in every way: desires for ever younger women and visions of hapless violence, murder, and suicide—all accompanied by increasingly sinister demons and fallen angels.

The bill collectors called. The repo men came. And I watched my life unravel. Of course, if one isn't paying one's bills, all this would be an expected outcome. But in some way I perceived that I was being loyal to the god of this world and expected different results. That was the deception. I expected Satan to take care of me in the flesh, and not just for sexual desire. I believed he had the power to bring earthly riches to me through my loyalty. There was a constant internal battle over my expectations and the outcomes. The result was deepening frustration, which produced greater anger.

Depression was constant. As my depression deepened, so did my hatred for God. This had been a running theme in my life: any hardship or setbacks caused me to shrink further away from the

God of truth and light that I didn't know and back to the god that, unfortunately, I knew too well. It wasn't really so much a choice as an innate response to the world I functioned in, a form of an entitlement mentality at its worst.

✝

Looking back, I can see that this dark lifestyle was a generational wooing. A satanic imprint had been etched into my spiritual DNA and handed down with an objective to invade generations to come, if allowed. Bottom line is this: I truly believed (and still do) that what was happening was a generational curse handed down in my family. Although I take full responsibility for deliberate choices I made to serve evil, there was a sort of satanic generational duress. It would be much like the child of an alcoholic becoming an alcoholic. I never experienced my parents practicing satanism, but their weak Christian-like practices, along with my mother's dabbling in psychic readers and such, led me to the conclusion that their trust and faith in the God of the universe was shallow and insubstantial.

I concluded that their God produced weak followers. That's all I knew for the most part growing up. How would I know this? Why didn't I surmise that I just hadn't met a strong believer yet? Looking back, I see that I had constant input from the adversary, who was taking over and directing my thought life in a sort of revelation knowledge that captivated my mind. It intrigued me with new questioning and deeper uncontrollable thoughts that led to unreasonable reasoning.

When I was obedient to Satan, he lavished power on me that made my flesh soar. For instance, as I have described, I seemed to gain more favor with the opposite sex. I had more women and greater experiences in the area of sexual desire. I saw vivid results from spells and incantations. I would pray for fires, and they would happen. For instance, a Christian prays for a friend needing a job, and the friend gets a job. The Christian has a praise report and gives God the glory. Similar things happen on the dark side: I prayed for evil things, and when the evil things happened, I gave Satan the glory. Whether it was merely circumstantial or even self-delusion didn't matter. A lot of action was happening around me, and I fashioned a sense of purpose for it all—evil purpose. For better or worse, there always was a stirring in the spirit for everything physical around me; everything became extraordinary and mysteriously significant.

When I was disobedient to what Satan wanted of me, the dark power stopped. Yet, once my flesh had become enticed, this left me in a state of perpetual craving. This was no more evident than when I sought opposing doctrines or opinions, especially a Christian influence. This would create a white-hot internal conflict that overflowed inside of me. I'd become a spiritual conduit carrying a diabolical influence that, if Satan's plans were not thwarted, would bring harm to many (and to me).

╫

As this battle for my soul continued, Christians became entangled in my life in ways that could now only be seen as divine in nature. Though the usual Mormons and Jehovah's Witnesses canvassed my new neighborhood, none would stop in to see me. They passed my house as if there were an unwritten law against stopping there. However one day, four people came up to my door from Faith Church, a local church. For reasons unknown to me at the time, I allowed them into my house. They came in, sat down, and spoke of God, Jesus, and the path to salvation. I listened.

The young man who led the conversation seemed a little apprehensive. Yet he spoke with boldness, and I listened. A woman with him was in constant silent prayer. The other two I didn't see. They were there, but my attention was on the young man and the slender woman who spoke silent words to a God she adored.

I noticed my attention span was lasting longer than ever before. As I reflected on the message the church members were trying to convey, the lava that usually churned inside of me seemed to subside. The more they spoke, the more I listened. The man asked me if I went to church. I explained to him my beliefs and where I had been spiritually. I was unable to lie to him as I became transfixed on the words that seemed to flow from his mouth like water from a fountain.

Mind games were my modus operandi in these situations, but I lost any desire to attempt to confuse them. Something had come over me. The two-hour conversation was unique to me at this time in my life. Their words about God seemed to bring clarity to my dark, tortured mind; I could think more clearly in their presence. Although I didn't give my heart over to their God, I did send them on their way with a few artifacts of my walk with Satan. I don't recall why I did so. They took a grocery sack full of satanic bibles, ritual knives, and altar pieces with them. I later learned they burned all the items and prayed over me and my household.

They'd hit the evangelical jackpot. Here they were, for the first time in their lives, witnessing to a real-life satanist who was open to change! What a jewel in their crowns this would bring.

✝

Later that week, my new sales manager, Cliff, came up from Dallas to work with me. I told him he could just spend the night with me instead of getting a hotel room. I wasn't aware he was a Christian, much less an associate pastor of a small church in his hometown. My radar had been temporarily shut down for some reason since my visit from the Faith Church clan, and I was off my game.

It was a heavy night in the spirit, and I sensed a lot of activity in and around my house. I noticed about three thirty in the morning that Cliff was on the phone to his wife. He was pacing back and forth in the bedroom I'd provided him, praying with his wife on the phone. I overheard him tell her that he had encountered spiritual resistance and demonic activity before, but these demons just would not go. He told his wife that the heaviness was about to crush his chest and he had to leave. The Lord had commanded him to leave. Within twenty minutes of the phone call, he was packed and on the road back to Dallas. He called me early the next day and asked me what I was into. When I told him, he fired me.

Now with more time on my hands, I was channel-surfing in bed one night when I came across a Larry King interview with Mark David Chapman, the man who assassinated the music legend John Lennon. I was intrigued with the story of his dark past; so much so, I began to send letters to him at Attica Prison in New York, where he was housed. He responded a month later, and it was not what I'd expected. After explaining the role that Satan had in my life, all Mark could share with me was his personal experience with Jesus Christ. He was a committed follower of the risen Savior, and he tried to guide me toward Him.

The visit from the church members, the correspondence with Mark David Chapman, and I'm sure the constant prayers of other concerned saints had begun to drip into my spirit. Despite the fact that I was steeped in dark-side fellowship and activities, I started to attend a local church a few times a month. In hindsight, although my motives may not have been pure, Edmond Church was a critical step in setting into motion a larger objective that was already at work in my life. Edmond Church was a nondenominational gathering of several thousand people. I went to a singles group there and actually behaved . . . for a while.

There was an experience at Edmond Church that will probably last me a lifetime. Once a month the church would have a concert with an internationally known singer/songwriter by the name of Dennis Jernigan; I ventured to it one time. I went there to possibly corrupt people, and I came into the foyer when a praise and worship song was playing. I tried to enter at intermission or a time when the music wasn't playing since I was definitely not into any kind of praise and worship. The song I heard as I hurried out of the foyer haunted me for years; I just could not get that melody out of my head. It was a song called "You Are My All in All."

I didn't like the pastor and cursed his ministry with demons of lust for both money and women. In other words, I prayed against this pastor and put spells on him and sent curses his way. I believed these curses did not go unheard. The pastor did eventually fall in several areas of his life. Perhaps it was his own pride and selfish desires that caused his demise; still, I took credit for his downfall. Was it my pride taking all the credit? Probably—but it could also be the dark powers I'd obtained coming to fruition.

In any case, I wanted to see the pastor fall and the church body weakened. My church attendance was a clear reflection of my double-mindedness. I had the capacity to be gracious, even kind, to people at church—but if someone hurt or angered me, I would retaliate with hatred. Curses and covert criminal activity were routine. I'd resort to petty vandalism. Once I even removed all the lug nuts off all four wheels on the car of a guy who'd "crossed" me— and the guy was a cop. It was a highly unstable period.

In spite of my darkened spiritual condition, I made friends, attended worship services, and managed to absorb some of the messages. In an attempt to deceive and get the Christians I knew to back off some, I was even baptized in front of the congregation. This was not a heartfelt event; I did it to ease the Christian overload. I didn't feel pressure to conform. It was more like "keeping your friends close and your enemies closer." I figured that once I was baptized, the church would leave me alone.

This was an example of something I had seen so often at church, and Satan had me exploit the "condition," if you will. Let me explain. What I witnessed quite often was Christians loving someone into the kingdom and their church; but once inside, the new believer was nearly abandoned. From a dark-side perspective, the battle began the minute the so-called new believer raised his hand. If not loved, mentored, or discipled for a period of time, the new believer, whether he is actually saved (depending on doctrine) or not, is ineffective for the kingdom and easy prey.

It was a strange and common occurrence that the church seemed oblivious to, but the adversary used as a commonplace battleground. My god was teaching me well how to distract, deceive, and divide believers. As I prayed to my god, he revealed these things. He delighted in and mocked the "church condition."

I was getting more in tune with my mission, and the training ground was inside the church.

✝

Gradually, in a small way, I felt the prayers of those I was sent to hurt starting to penetrate and dismantle some of my foundational thought processes. The more I was around the believers at Edmond Church and their prayers, the more I began to second-guess my way and my god. Although many might see this as a breakthrough and desire for freedom from my satanic lifestyle, I did not intend to relent and convert to their God and way. Christianity still seemed a weaker spiritual path than what I had. There was too much immediate gratification and too many feelings of power in the dark way. Their God didn't seem to give them any power, just demands for flaky kindness and back-slapping Christian cheer. Nevertheless, something was getting through to my hard heart, and at times, I didn't know whether to embrace it or run from it.

There was an old song I used to listen to a lot that reinforced a deep conviction of mine. It was from the Rolling Stones: "Sympathy for the Devil." The more satanic my belief system, the more I felt sorry for Satan. *You mean to tell me he was in heaven and God kicked him out? Why? Because he rebelled? Couldn't God reprimand him in another way than eternal damnation?* In my mind, the crime didn't justify the punishment, and that reinforced my thoughts, justification, and pursuit of the dark world. I felt sorry for the devil and his rebellious nature.

In America we are taught to question authority, to be independent thinkers, to do our own thing . . . and the list goes on. I felt like the James Dean of the Christian church—I was going to roll up my sleeves and take the fight to them in their own camp! I was not only responsible for my actions; I was proud of them. Could it be that my anger was not as much due to my own tragic life circumstances as it was my sacrifice of self to get even with a God who, in my thinking, had unjustly punished one-third of the heavenly host? *This is one victim that God cannot get*, I would say to myself. *I am not going to serve a God like that.*

☩

One of the Bible verses I heard at Edmond Church said, "Light has come into the world, but people loved darkness instead of light because their deeds were evil. Everyone who does evil hates the light, and will not come into the light for fear that their deeds will be exposed" (John 3:19–20). This passage defined my life. I would come far enough into the light to get a little relief from my torment and then walk right back to the darkness to indulge my sin. This same, unrepentant pattern took me to the end of my rope and left me both physically and mentally exhausted. At this very low point, I made another acquaintance that would impact my life.

Gerald Deaton was a godly man who took great interest in my life. He invited me to his church, and I agreed to go purely out of respect for Gerald.

On my first Sunday in Gerald's church, I showed up for worship service, and a few minutes into the service, I felt as if my heart were being torn out. Anxious, conflicted, and nervous, I had to hurry out of the crowded sanctuary twice to throw up in the men's room. When I tried to go back into the sanctuary, I became nauseous. It felt like the flu, but I knew better. The spiritual forces of darkness increasingly controlled me, and I gave in to them and left the church.

I would define this period as "heavy" in the spirit. I was bent on disruption of all things holy, and Satan had set my sights on my local churches and Bible study groups. I went to services and Bible studies from about fifteen local churches and did all that was in me to disrupt them spiritually. Once in the group, I would twist Scripture in order to cause confusion and start arguments. One example is James 4:7, which says, "Submit yourselves, then, to God. Resist the devil, and he will flee from you." In a group of unknowledgeable believers, I would throw out the phrase "Resist the devil, and he will flee!" Sounds right-on and harmless, but it is far from the truth. These people would go on about their business, thinking if they just resisted the devil when they felt oppression, they would be okay. I didn't tell them the most important portion of that scripture: "Submit yourselves, then, to God." That is the crux of that verse. The adversary is going nowhere unless one is in submission to God! And even then, there may still be a fight.

My end goal was anything that took the believers' minds off spiritual matters and onto worldly matters. This kept my diabolical mission of misleading and leading Christians away from their faith moving forward, sharpened my manipulative powers, and provided a little amusement. I was booted out of a few study groups and banned from several churches during this period of my life.

A shocking revelation for me during my "predatory" period was the number of people I encountered in churches and study groups who were completely lost, regardless of denomination. They simply were not committed to the pursuit of God. Most groups had one person who was truly seeking God, but the general lack of depth and understanding of other participants stood out. They were misinformed, often uninformed, and their lack of knowledge made them easy targets for Satan. Their vulnerabilities didn't stop with spiritual ignorance. If I was looking for an easy sexual conquest, I could usually find a willing female participant at home groups and churches. I soon discovered it was easier to find sex in a home group filled with ignorant believers or the seeking lost than it was in a local bar.

There were, however, some exceptions to this general rule. One night, I went to the south side of Oklahoma City to go to a home group of believers from a Vineyard church. When I arrived, I sensed that this wasn't the typical group I'd visited year after year. Probably ten people were in attendance, a mix of both men and women, nothing out of the ordinary. However, I did notice a couple of men who seemed to be anointed or protected more than I had seen in a while. This spiritual hedge around them piqued my curiosity.

A young Christian named Herbert seemed to sense some of the evil present around me, and we got into something of a spiritual staredown. He was discerning and bright but seemed young in his faith and fluctuated between the spirit and the flesh. Our little skirmish managed to disrupt the flow of the study. Another man in attendance, Jim Kimbrough, displayed a gentle and loving spirit, and he reprimanded Herbert for his attempts to do spiritual battle in this setting. I sensed a special anointing on Jim and was immediately attracted to what he had. And as I look back, Jim did the kindest thing a believer can do for another person: he loved his way into my life.

Soon, I invited Jim over for dinner. He met my three children, and we got along well. Over time, I shared my dark story with Jim, and even though I was not saved, within a few months he asked me to be the best man at his upcoming wedding. Despite my spiritual darkness, Jim wove himself into the frayed fabric of my life.

Even as I was experiencing a relational breakthrough, the rest of my life was continually disintegrating. Behind on rent and struggling financially, I was stalked by depression. I dropped out of school and tried to find some construction work. The only immediate work I could find was in Las Vegas, helping an acquaintance build an addition to a church recreation hall. So I went to Nevada for work that should have lasted a couple of months. I was promised a nice sum of money for the job, but after a few weeks, the contractor absconded with the money and left many holding the bag. As an addicted gambler, whenever he came across any money, it went to feed that monster. He also had another addiction: cocaine. I wanted to stay away from both.

So when my daughter Marisa called and asked me if I would attend her state swim meet back in Oklahoma, I left the job site, filled my gas tank, and left the hot desert sun of "sin city."

CHAPTER 5

THE JAILHOUSE WAY

*Again I looked and saw all the oppression that was
taking place under the sun: I saw the tears of the
oppressed—and they have no comforter; power was on
the side of their oppressors—and they have no comforter.
And I declared that the dead, who had already died, are
happier than the living, who are still alive. But better
than both is the one who has never been born, who has
not seen the evil that is done under the sun.*

—ECCLESIASTES 4:1–3

Without a dime to my name, I made it back to Oklahoma by stealing gas. I pulled into gas stations, pumped fuel, and when the attendant was distracted, drove off. Frustrating, yes, embarrassing, sure; but I needed to get home to my daughter.

It was mid-October, the day of her swim meet, when I arrived. A talented swimmer, Marisa had been competing for several years.

Marisa gave me a hug when I entered the gym and asked if I could officiate at the timing tables as I had before. Feeling good about reconnecting with my daughter and excited about her race, I was assigned a lane and began my duties. Over three hundred people attended this all-day statewide event.

I was timing a swimmer when I felt a tap on my shoulder. I turned around to see a sheriff's deputy staring at me.

"Are you Michael Leehan?"

I nodded.

"This is a summons for you to appear in court for failure to pay child support." I stared at the document in my hand as humiliation hit me right in the gut. "You have been served, Mr. Leehan." He turned on his heels and walked away as I sat dumbfounded, looking for something to crawl under and hide my shame.

The new deadbeat dad laws had just taken effect, and my ex-wife, with the help of her high-priced attorney, had picked this time to disgrace me in front of my children and the crowd. When Marisa climbed out of the pool with her eyes wide and her hand over her mouth, I felt it was a new low for me and my daughter. She approached me at the table with equal parts embarrassment and concern.

"Dad, what . . . what happened?" She laid her hand on my shoulder. I looked up at her and all I could manage to say was, "I'm sorry, honey."

☩

Two days later, I was in the Oklahoma County courthouse, waiting to appear before the judge. Just before I got to the courtroom, I received a phone call from a new customer who wanted me to build a room addition. This job would pay well enough for me to catch up on my back child support payments and allow me to find a place to live. What are the odds? An unexpected phone call saves the day. Believing I'd caught a break, I told my customer I would meet him at 2 p.m. for an advance on the job and start the following day. Problem solved: get the advance, pay my ex-wife, get out of trouble, easy fix. But I was wrong.

Soon after that phone call, I was called into the courtroom. As I stood in front of the judge, he asked me, "Mr. Leehan, do you have an attorney to represent you?"

"No sir."

He then asked, "Do you have the child support arrearage you are ordered to pay?"

"No, I do not," I answered. "Your honor, I do have a new—"

"I don't want to hear another word," the judge snapped. "You are remanded to the Oklahoma County jail, where you will remain until December 22—unless you can post a cash bond of $14,567. At that time, you will be given your day in my court to face the charges of contempt of court for failure to pay your court-ordered child support. Enjoy your stay, Mr. Leehan." I stared at the judge with all the venom I could muster. He gave me no opportunity to explain, no chance to tell him I'd have the money in a few weeks, no chance for redemption.

Handcuffed in court by a sheriff's deputy, I was escorted from the fifth floor of the courtroom through the lobby to a prisoner van parked outside the complex. At the jail, I was placed in a holding cell with fifteen other inmates to await processing. Within four hours, I was medically examined, had a body cavity search, had mug shots taken, and had an inmate number assigned—I was ready to be taken to the prison cell that would be my home for the next two months.

Facing time in jail should have scared me, but it didn't. My life was already a chaotic mess with mounting debt, repo men, the long arm of the law, my ex-wife grinding on me, and the stress and disorder that came from practicing the dark arts. In comparison, jail offered relief. All I had to do was learn the language, the unwritten rules, and the hierarchy of my new world, and I would survive.

✝

After being processed, I was assigned to a pod that would be my home for the next few months. A pod is an enclosed portion of a floor (level) that houses fifty inmates. Each floor of the complex had four pods. Floors of the jail complex housed inmates based on the level of crimes committed. Guys who failed to pay child support, in most cases, wouldn't be housed with a guy who murdered a family of three. As luck would have it, my first pod contained forty-nine felons and me. I came to find out my new "neighbors" had been responsible for a total of thirty-five murders. These young gangbangers lived by their own codes and were fiercely loyal to each other.

I began to assimilate to the "jailhouse way." I shaved my head, grew a beard, and secluded myself from the others. I began a fast that would last thirty days. (Satanists fast for the same reasons Christians do—to bring greater clarity, strength, and power—but for all the wrong motives.) I gave my food to some of the gangbangers who were hungry, and they helped conceal my fast. I didn't want to draw attention and knew this would serve a few of my intentions.

The first three days are the toughest of any kind of fast; after that time, not eating gets easier. Having power over one's flesh actually gives strength to one's spirit, regardless of which god one serves. The hungrier I became and the more my stomach ached, the more my spirit came alive. A time came that, out of habit and perhaps sheer force of will, I didn't think about food anymore.

Random thoughts turned into ideas about business I would conduct when released, visions of my kids, and watching my back. Spiritual power and insight increased, and conquering my flesh gave me courage.

My fellow inmates reacted differently to me than to the others in the pod. Like animals in cages, criminals sense fear immediately in this environment. Weak and strong exist together, and it often has nothing to do with physical size. While starving my flesh, my spirit was being empowered by dark forces that made me a man not to be messed with. The men I came into contact with might not have been well educated, but their "street smarts" were intact; in this environment, they needed those in order to survive.

Most of the men in jail didn't use proper names; they had nicknames based on their cell. Each of the four pods per floor has a letter—A, B, C, D—and the fifty cells per pod are numbered. So "829C" referred to a young, black gangbanger I got to know: eighth floor, C pod, cell 29. To him, I was "850C," or "50" for short; I called him "29." Cold, hard, and impersonal—that was as close as most of us would get to each other.

Upon meeting him, I stared at 29 for a few seconds, sized him up, and then nodded. "Okay, 29, you can take my food . . . just don't say a word. I don't want to attract attention," I told him, looking around the mess hall.

Then 29 shook his head, and said, "You tryin' to kill yourself? I haven't seen you eat a scrap of food in days. Man, they may be onto you."

I answered, "Nah, nothin' like that, just trying to take control of something. See, if you can control something you crave, it only makes you stronger." I tapped my forehead with my index finger. "Real strength is in here. You want to control your environment . . . you control this first."

He looked at me as if I had two heads. "Man, that's heavy talk for a bald-headed white dude. You're not tryin' to get in my head?"

I smiled at 29 and chuckled.

"Okay, then." And 29 quickly scraped my food onto his tray.

"You been down awhile, huh?" I said to him.

"Yup, awhile," he said. "What about you? What's your story?"

I looked at him with eyes as hard as marbles. "You wouldn't believe me if I told you. Anyway, it's a long one."

He pointed his finger at me. "You killed someone. I see it in your eyes. You're a killer." Then 29 took a big bite of a roll and did a hard swallow. "Crazy white boy killer, that's what you is."

"My father, the one I now serve, sent me here."

"So you killed your old man?"

"Uh-uh . . . more like, he killed me."

At that, 29 twisted up his face. "Man, I never heard nobody talkin' like this. You just nuts, is all you is . . . man. Anyway, crazy old white dude, can I have your trays if you're not eatin' for a while?" He looked behind to see if his "crew" was watching his back.

I smelled the fear emanating from his body. "Yeah, 29, you can have them. But it's our secret, right?" I said. He nodded and hurried back to his boys.

The next twenty-six days went the same. When 29 came to my cell at mealtime, he brought me his empty tray, and I handed him my untouched one. The guards never knew the difference.

On the day my fast was over, 29 came to my cell as usual. He saw me lying on my bunk with my feet up, an empty tray on my table.

"Hey, 50, where yo' extras?" he asked.

I didn't make eye contact with him, but I pointed to the empty tray. "My fast is over . . . no extras."

I watched 29 squint and put on his hard-edged gangster look. He came over and shoved my foot off the rail I'd propped it on. "Nah, 50, I don't think it's over . . . Cuz, who gonna give me extras, if you don't?"

I didn't move for a second. He kicked my other foot. I jumped up and stood about two inches from his face. "I think I just told you, no more extras." He backed down. "In fact, 29, you ever look at me again in here, bad things are gonna happen to you."

He stared at me, trying to hold his ground, but getting more scared by the second. Then 29 walked away. We never spoke again.

Except for my contact with 29, I kept a low profile for the first few weeks inside, but boredom eventually got the best of me. Anyway, Satan had made me a dedicated rabble-rouser. I knew it was time to stir something up with my new neighbors. My paranoia knew no limitations, and I began to take notes during lockdown on the other inmates I met, breaking down conversations, looking for weaknesses and ways to exploit my new "friends."

My first cell mate, Eric, a young white boy from some backwater town, had murdered his mom and stepfather. He hid on top of their mobile home with a deer rifle and shot them both when they were coming home one night. He said, "I hated my mom for leaving my dad. And my stepdad was mean to me . . . so I just shot 'em." I did a double take on Eric as he was telling me his story, impressed with his level of detachment over a cold-blooded act. I was looking Eric over again, when suddenly the cell door opened.

"Hey, Leehan, you have a visitor," the guard yelled. "Come on."

I entered a room with small cubicles and a heavy glass partition that could stop a bullet. This partition separated the criminals from the family and friends who came to visit. My mother sat on the other side of the glass and stared at me as if I were a stranger.

I stared back and finally spoke: "Hi, Mom."

She continued to stare at my new jailhouse look (I had shaved my head and had a goatee), then said, "Son, you look like the devil."

I laughed. My mom didn't know what I was into spiritually. For her to say this to me was almost a compliment. For a moment, I wondered if she knew what I had been up to on the outside before I came to my new home here. *Nah, she doesn't have the gift*, I thought. But how ironic that she said that to me . . .

"Some of these guys in here think I am the devil," I said.

"I barely recognized you, son. Are you taking care of yourself?" she asked.

I smiled. "Doing the best I can under the circumstances, Mom." Disappointment clouded her eyes. She couldn't mask her displeasure, and it was still a bitter pill for me to swallow.

She shut her eyes, opened them slowly, then continued, "Well, it's the holidays, and I wanted to come by and say merry Christmas."

"Well, merry Christmas to you too."

"It sure is a long wait to get back here. They had me waiting for two hours to get back here to see you."

"I know it's inconvenient, but I appreciate you coming." Our conversation felt forced, awkward.

Mom stared at me. I knew she had something she wanted to get off her chest and braced myself for what was coming. "Son, you should have just left those kids and moved away. That woman you married was a disaster, and I knew she would bring you down. I know the type, and she's one of them. She was either going to have you hurt or make sure you ended up in here. And, well, here you are," she said into the phone.

"Ah, it's all good, Mom. I'm surviving and in some ways a little relieved to be in here."

She looked at me oddly as she absorbed those words. I felt a flood of emotions wash over me as I looked at my mother and considered how badly she failed me and how she sat there thinking how badly I'd failed her.

"Why didn't you come to court?" I asked her. "I didn't have a single family member there to support me."

My mom looked a little sheepish. Looking back, I am glad she was not at court. It would have been another person I would have had to stare at in shame.

"Well, son, it was a difficult time for all of us, as I'm sure you can understand, a hard time."

"Well, I can tell you about hard time." I could tell she was embarrassed by her comment. "Doesn't really matter anyway. I got what I deserved—right, Mom?" She said nothing. "And like I said, I'm almost glad to be in here. I was headed down the wrong path. I was into some strange stuff, Mom. With this kind of depression, you can get yourself in a lot of trouble out there."

"Do they give you medicine in here?"

"No. What's the use? There's not enough medication in the state of Oklahoma to keep someone from being depressed in this dump. Anyway, merry Christmas, Mom."

"Can I do anything? You look thin, son." She looked concerned. "Are you losing weight?"

"Aw, the food here isn't worth eating," I replied.

"What's that bruise on the side of your face?"

"I ran into the edge of my cell door, not looking. You know, clumsy old me. Listen, don't feel obligated to come back. I know it's a major hassle."

I hung up the phone and stood to let the guard know I was through. I waved good-bye to my mother through the glass. She took one last look at me—her son, the jailbird, the convict who couldn't pay his child support, who seemed to be falling headlong into the arms of failure—and she seemed mostly annoyed. What I remember most about this moment with my mom is what she did not say: no "I love you" or "I'm so sorry" or "Please forgive me for not being at your court date."

Even in my darkened condition, my mother's capacity to make me feel like a failure burned deeply. Nothing can inflict pain quite like family.

I glanced back at my mom as she gathered her purse to leave. She didn't look back. I didn't see her for another year.

✝✝

My good fortune with roommates continued when Lawrence came into my life. A Sammy Davis Jr. lookalike, Lawrence would have been kind of comical had he not been an institutionalized criminal. Lawrence had spent about thirty years in prison on a manslaughter charge and was about to be released. Lawrence rattled on nonstop the minute he came into my cell. His main objective was to intimidate me.

He claimed to have an aunt deep into witchcraft. He said she owned a big white wolf, and if I ever hacked him off, he'd have her put a spell on me. Lawrence was crazy and dangerous; little did he know, however, that he was barking up the wrong tree in the subject of witchcraft.

Lawrence was assigned to my cell because of a fight with a previous roommate. The story I got from Lawrence as he was unpacking his stuff was, "My last roommate, he snored loud. I got sick of it, so I finally choked and nearly killed him with a towel." Lawrence was eyeing me, checking out my fear factor, seeing how I reacted. I let his words hang in the air for a minute.

"Guess what, Lawrence? I snore too," I said.

Lawrence glared at me then said, "You do it very long, and I will cut you up."

I stood up slowly, looked at Lawrence dead in the eye, and said evenly, "Blades don't scare me. I always sleep with one eye open."

When I wasn't fasting, I would get candy from the commissary and hide it in my cell. While I took showers or was away from the cell, Lawrence would rifle through my stuff and take whatever he wanted, thinking he could push me around.

One day I caught him stealing and said, "Get your hands off my stuff!"

Lawrence looked up with a handful of my stashed candy. "White boy, you better watch yo' mouth . . ."

"Get your punk self outta my stash," I barked. I placed a heavy emphasis on the *punk* part because of a story Lawrence had shared with me. While he was down (a term used for imprisoned) for thirty years, he had a "girlfriend" named Cocoa. She was his dream girl (guy).

I had said, "You're homosexual, then?"

He sneered at me. "Nah, it's jus' what you do when you're down."

I told him there was no way that I would do that. I told him he was a punk. So I stood there calling him a punk again, until his blood boiled.

"I'm gonna cut you up, white boy. It's comin'," he threatened.

My laughter sent him over the edge. He couldn't stand to be mocked, and being trapped in a six-by-ten-foot cell with me only frustrated him.

This trash talk raged on for a few restless nights, and the tension grew between us. One night, with tempers on edge, I knew it was on. Lawrence had hidden a razor blade in the mattress. I had stuffed one of my socks full of batteries, some small rocks I found stashed in the pod, and a few bars of soap.

Lights-out was 10 p.m. Lawrence got in the bunk below me and tossed and turned awhile. He acted like he was going to sleep, but I knew he was just "playing possum" before he made his move. I stayed alert and listened as a couple of hours crept by. Then Lawrence's mattress springs squeaked as he rose from his bunk.

I had my sock hammer ready and swung it over the edge of my bunk and struck him in the head. He wasn't hurt badly but was slowed down in his attempt to use the razor blade. I jumped down off my bunk and went at him with my sock hammer. End result, I called the guards over the cell intercom. They took Lawrence to the infirmary. They took me to isolation and the next day to an inquiry. Since he'd had earlier problems with his roommates and I was a misdemeanor, I was off the hook. In truth, many of the guards were happy about my putting a beatdown on Lawrence. It was a racial issue, and the mostly white guards didn't like the loudmouthed black guy.

✝✝

I waited two months for my day in court. When that day finally arrived, I was driven from the county jail with several other inmates who were on the same docket. Emotionally, things had only worsened inside, and I managed to drag my wretched attitude into court with me.

I arrived in court handcuffed, wearing an orange jumpsuit and blue slip-on sneakers. To my surprise the room was packed, and the first people I noticed were my ex-wife and her husband, Chuck. The problem compounded since several of her family members, some of whom lived in nearby states, were there as well. From the back row, Chuck sneered at me.

After all the problems I'd had in my life to this point, being humiliated in court in front of ex-relatives was a new low. I saw them on the back row, salivating over the prospect of my getting the book thrown at me. I sat trapped in this state of utter humiliation for about two hours until my name was called:

"The State of Oklahoma versus Mr. Michael Anthony Leehan," said the judge.

"Here, Your Honor." I rose to my feet.

"You may approach the bench. Do you have counsel, Mr. Leehan?" he asked.

"I do not," I answered.

I approached the bench with the eyes of my ex and her family trained on me. As I came to a stop in front of the judge, I heard Chuck's mocking laughter from the back row. I was joined in front by a well-dressed attorney whom I quickly realized was my ex-wife's counsel hired by her family. Like a lamb being led to slaughter, I looked up and faced the judge.

"Mr. Leehan, you are here to face the charges of contempt of court. Do you understand these charges?"

"I do, Your Honor. But since I'm being charged with a crime, isn't it my right to have counsel supplied to me by the state?" I asked. "I am indigent and request a public defender."

The judge looked less than sympathetic. "Yes, Mr. Leehan, please explain why you believe the State of Oklahoma should pay for your defense, and I will listen."

"First of all, it's my constitutional right, Your Honor. I'm broke. I can't work due to severe depression, and I need counsel. My depression is a documented medical fact. I have physicians who can verify this fact and—"

"Mr. Leehan," the judge interrupted. "I don't like your attitude." The judge stared down at me as I heard more snickers from good ol' Chuck in the back row.

This was not going well. The judge examined some papers as my life and my future slipped away.

Finally, the judge said, "Mr. Leehan, the State of Oklahoma will provide you with counsel." A sense of relief washed over me, as I watched the judge thumb through his papers. The judge continued, "Let me look at my docket and see when I have time for you to return." The judged looked at some papers and then stared down at me with eyes cold and unmerciful. "Okay, it looks like February will work."

It was December. The judge was using his docket to coerce me into waiving my constitutional rights. I could either waive my rights and take my chances in court that day, or I could spend another two months in the county jail.

Failure to pay child support is a serious issue, but it was only a misdemeanor violation at this point. The maximum I could receive would be a year in jail. If I waited to see him again with a public defender (or "public pretender," as they called them in the jail), I could get the maximum sentence, plus the two months already served, and the additional two months to wait for the judge's docket opening. I'm sure most of us have to make important decisions on the fly in life, but this was a biggie. At worst, I would get twelve additional months representing myself on the spot, or I could wait on a public defender and possibly face fourteen months in jail.

That famous quote from Abraham Lincoln comes to mind: "A man who represents himself has a fool for a client." Well, this fool shot back to the judge, "Your Honor, I guess I am here pro se." (*Pro se* is a legal term meaning "self-represented without an attorney present" . . . in other languages, it means "idiot").

As the judge was writing something on his notepad, he barked back at me, "Watch your mouth in my courtroom, Mr. Leehan."

Knowing the deck was stacked against me and I was about to get the shaft, I gave my *up yours* to the judge and muttered something derogatory, thinking the judge could not hear me.

The judge's face turned a deep crimson color. He didn't respond but just wrote something on a notepad. I assume he was calculating how long he could incarcerate me under the law. "Well, Mr. Leehan, I'm dying to hear the reasons you failed so miserably to provide for your children."

I started rattling off my history of depression and inability to find steady work because of my mental state, and on I went, like the fool of a client I'd made myself, until the judge had had enough.

"Is that all, Mr. Leehan?" the judge asked.

I knew my career as a defense attorney was going to be short lived, so I threw in the towel. "Yes, it is," I said. Of all the self-destructive things a guy can do, hacking off a judge when you're standing in his courtroom ranks high on that list. There I stood, watching the judge's face turn red and his eyes become narrow and flinty.

"Very well, then. I sentence you to eight months for contempt of court to be served in the Oklahoma County Jail. Time already served does not apply"—which means I got a ten-month sentence—"and there will be no 'good time' allowed."

You've heard the expression "getting the book thrown at you"? Well, the judge just knocked me upside the head with one the size of the *American Heritage Dictionary*. This sentence meant that no matter how well I behaved, I couldn't get out any sooner.

When his gavel came down, the judge informed me that I'd be going back to county jail. I wouldn't see the sun for the next eight months. My hot temper, loud mouth, and disdain for authority had cost me big. *What an idiot*, I thought. *I'm only behind on child support, and I'm handcuffed to a guy who killed a family of three.* But because of pride, arrogance, and an inability to control my tongue, I was in league with real criminals and separated from my kids.

I know it's hypocritical for a guy to feel treated unjustly by this little court of the world, all the while being guilty before the "court of the universe" as a henchman of the devil. I knew in my heart how guilty I was in so many areas of my life. It was also ironic that I was going to jail for such a minor offense in comparison to some of the crimes against society I had secretly committed.

I thought the walk of shame I took coming into the courtroom was tough. It was nothing compared to my exit. I avoided eye contact with everyone, especially my former family and Chuck. As the accused murderer and I paraded past, once again I heard Chuck laughing.

The man I was handcuffed to leaned into me and said, "If I were you, when I got outta jail, I'd slit his throat, my man."

I took his advice a little too seriously, as taking Chuck out would become a priority of mine in the not-too-distant future.

Once again, I was driven back to the place I would be living for the next eight months.

†

I'd been in jail about two more months when letters started coming. Not long after that, visitors came. Jim Kimbrough, Gerald Deaton, Don Nusbaum, a local prison minister (whose name I do not recall), Dwayne Jaynes, and some other Christian men visited me. In time, I began to reject all visitors, as they reminded me too much of the outside world. Thinking about life on the outside and what you were missing made time stand still. I lived hour by hour, day by day, and didn't want anything to make my stay more difficult.

After four months of filing cop-out slips, I became a trustee and was moved to the second floor of the complex. (A cop-out slip is a form inmates fill out to request a transfer, legal or administrative assistance, or any type of personal attention.) Rules in the trustee pod were more relaxed, and the inmates had more liberty. We had access to games, TV, and showers almost anytime we chose. Lights-out was at midnight. Life here was much easier since everyone had earned trustee status and most were only misdemeanor offenders. This was a far cry from the "murderer's row" where I'd lived the past four months. These guys were all short-timers with freedom within reach.

I was assigned to laundry and went there every day to fold

uniforms, separate women's and men's clothes, and serve on the mobile team that distributed clothes and bedsheets to the prisoners. Every day we took blankets and uniforms to a couple of floors. Some days were more interesting than others. I reveled in giving blue blankets to the Bloods and red blankets to the Crips. Both are street gangs and have colors associated with their respective gangs—Bloods are red and Crips are blue. The ultimate disrespect was to give them colors of their rival gang. This amounted to a capital offense in their world. I'm certain I'd be dead right now had I stayed in jail much longer, because both gangs hated me. Every time I stepped in that pod, profanity flew in my direction.

One time Slim, a white guard who'd become my friend, was on duty as we passed out clothes. The protocol was for me to drop an inmate's clothes by the door of his cell and back away against a wall, while the officer in charge opened the cell door and handed the inmate his clothes. This time I didn't obey.

A Crip about my size hated me and acted like a tough guy behind the locked cell door. I threw down the usual red blanket with his clothes. He yelled at me through the door. Slim wasn't paying attention (or just wanted to see what would happen) and turned his back to me. When the door opened, I rushed in behind him and fought with this lone Crip. It was pure exhilaration. Physically the match was pretty even, but he would have eventually whipped me had Slim not been there, as the Crip was much younger and had more stamina.

This event represented the insanity that my life had become under Satan: a thirtysomething white guy eagerly getting into a brawl with a black teenage gangster in county jail just for the thrill of it. I had little fear of anything physical, as I knew from past experience that power lay in the spiritual. But when you bottom out as I had, you stop caring about a whole lot. The fact that I had no regard for my own safety was more an indication of my lack of self-respect than a mark of bravery.

Slim had called for backup when the fight began in case the situation got out of hand. A guard named Crawley came to assist. After Crawley pulled me away from the incident, he took me away from the pod and back to my cell. Crawley was a well-muscled black guard who would eventually become a friend during my incarceration.

"C'mon, 50, you need to come with me," Crawley barked. "What are you thinking?"

"Ah, you know, it was something to do," I said, panting.

Crawley shook his head in disbelief, then said, "You know, I deal with all kinds in here: guys who have been down, guys going down, and real hard-core criminals. I've seen 'em all, but you really scare me. I can't put my hand on it, but there is just something about you that makes my hair stand up. I can read men, Mike. I can look in somebody's eyes and tell what they're about. I can tell if they're crazy, a pervert, flat-out mean, or a killer. But yours are different. There's something stirring behind your eyes, something I'm not sure about. Something dark, boy."

"It's sounds like we're not going to be able to date in here, then, huh?" I answered.

"Dude, shut up. Get your crazy butt in your cell and calm down."

"Crazy, huh? Is that what I am, Crawley . . . crazy?"

I took a seat in my cell as Crawley took a look over his shoulder to see what was going on behind us, then continued, "*Crazy* may not be the right word, but it's a scary crazy. Like I said, there's something about you I'm not familiar with."

"Can knowledge make you crazy, Crawley?"

He looked at me curiously.

"I mean, someone who has knowledge about things that most people don't—wouldn't that person seem a little crazy?"

Crawley cocked his head to the side and looked off in the distance for a moment. "Lemme think on that," he said. He turned toward the door.

"Hey, Crawley." He looked over at me.

"Yeah, 50."

"In the end, it's our decision what we choose to think about, isn't it? What we fill our minds with is a personal decision."

Crawley nodded. "Yeah, I believe that's right."

"Most people don't want real knowledge, because once you have it, you're obligated to do something with it. You're held accountable. Isn't that what you Christians believe?"

"50, how'd you know I was a believer?"

"It's your eyes, dude. Same reason you're spooked by mine. The eyes tell the whole story . . . the window to the soul, right? We can deceive ourselves all we want, but two forces are at work in this world, and two only. Having knowledge of one of those two forces is where the real power is."

"I know where my power comes from, 50 . . . How 'bout you?" Crawley said.

"I know I've been given real knowledge of things that aren't of this world . . . And power, well, it seems to be coming."

"Chill, man, or your head will explode. Four months and some change and you will be outta here. I hope you don't come back here like the rest of these fools." Crawley glanced around the cell. "You got nothing to read in here?" I shook my head. "Can I bring you a New Testament? The jail supplies them."

"Sure, I'll look at it. You can bring me a soda and a large order of fries while you're at it." I grinned at him.

"I'm prayin' for you, 50, but you stay the heck outta trouble. These guys don't play in here. They're ruthless, and they're all related. Like a big pack of animals."

"I can handle myself, dude."

"Yeah, you think you can. It's still dangerous in here for you. Last time I checked, you aren't about to win any popularity contests either, especially with the gangbangers." He looked at me, and I nodded.

Crawley continued, "You got some energy coming off of you, and it always leads you into trouble. Something is always goin' on around you, and it's not good. You need to get into God's Word, my man. That is a certainty. Do good time. You got four months, 50, four months . . ."

About an hour later I heard my cell door unlock. It was Crawley. He looked me in the eyes as he silently handed me a small brown paperback book. On the front of the book was marked *New Testament*. I held the book in my hand and stared at it. I really had little to say and was surprised that Crawley had come back so quickly.

Without words, Crawley exited and the cell door was shut and locked. I set the Bible on the stainless lavatory sink/toilet and sat down on my bunk. I stayed on my bunk for nearly an hour, wondering what I would do with that little book. After a great deal of thought, I decided what made the most sense to me was to memorize as much Scripture as I could, twist it and manipulate it, and throw it back to the jailhouse preachers I was housed with. There were many of them on the twelve or so floors, the guys trying to "pimp" God by feigning Christianity to the guards

and fellow inmates and judges just to get released. So I memorized Scripture and went out daily to agitate the efforts of the
mini-ministers. After memorization, I would also use the pages
as paper to roll homemade cigarettes to sell to other inmates. A
supply of these small Bibles was readily available from the guards.
These New Testaments could also be found strewn about on the
eating tables in each pod and in trash cans throughout the facility, discarded by hopeless incarcerates.

I not only desecrated the Scripture and played mind games
with Christians, but I also liked to rile the professed nonbelievers
and Muslim inmates I was housed with. It didn't take much to
get these guys upset. My favorite game with them was at night.
After lights went out and everyone was either trying to rest or
were on their "toilet phones," talking to their cousins on the
various floors, I would whistle the song "Amazing Grace" under
my cell door. A proficient whistler, I'd whistle a very bluesy
version of it over and over until I tired of hearing profane and
murderous speech directed at me, the whistler. Of course, no
one knew who the whistler was. They never quite figured out
my game.

Another incident occurred on the tenth floor in the high-
security pod. Here were dangerous offenders who could hurt or
kill a trustee or a guard if given the chance, so doors were not to
be opened. This procedure also prevented a trustee from slipping
contraband to one of the high-security inmates. The only cells
we could ever enter were empty, when an inmate was in court or
at the infirmary.

I'd gotten to know the guys on this floor well. Tom in 10C15
had murdered a family of four in Tennessee and a family of three
in Oklahoma. He was up on trial and was destined for death in

Tennessee. On his door was a sign that read: "Do not open door without at least four guards present and one white shirt." *White shirt* was a term used for a sergeant or ranking officer. Slim was the guard on duty and wasn't the fighting type.

I went up to Tom's door, and we greeted each other as normal. He was a big guy. I didn't notice him staring past me as he watched one of the trustee inmates on our clothing distribution team stealing from an inmate's empty cell and hiding the loot in the dirty clothes basket. Stealing from an inmate when he was gone was the ultimate form of disrespect. To my shock and horror, Tom's door gently eased open. (It must have been jimmied.) When the door opened, I froze.

Tom said, "Mike, you're a good man. Go in my cell and get out of this mess."

"Yes sir," I replied and would have snapped off a salute if I'd had time. The respect I'd earned from Tom over the last few months saved me.

Tom was in Slim's face before Slim could radio for help. He told Slim to give him the radio and that if he were smart he would join me on his bunk. Slim was eager to oblige. Tom then went over to the rest of the crew and administered one of the most ferocious beatings I'd ever witnessed. He pounded those men unmercifully. He sent all of them to the infirmary, and I'm not so sure one of them didn't die. When Tom finished, he came back to his cell panting, asked Slim and me to leave, and closed his door. The savagery of the beating he put on the trustees is as memorable as the courtesy he showed Slim and me. A code did exist. Honor among thieves was real. This was a strange world to occupy, even for a satanist.

Being on the distribution crew had its benefits. I would take commissary to guys who didn't have the privilege and sell panties I obtained in the laundry to the gay guys in protective custody. The going rate was three goodies (Twinkies, ramen noodles, candy bars, etc.) per pair. It didn't take long before I had a store in my cell. These items sold two for three to guys who were hungry and waiting on money to be put on their books. In other words, I would give them two items on credit, and they would have someone on the outside put money on my books in return, or would pay me back with three items when they could afford it.

If a guy wanted two items, I would take orders as I went around distributing clothes and would deliver them on my next time up (I was on the bottommost floor of the jail). I also sold snipes (illegal cigarettes made from tobacco of regular cigarettes discarded by the guards). A typical cigarette makes four snipes. The paper I used to make the cigarettes came from the pages of the New Testament supplied by Crawley. Nightly I would tear out a page, insert the tobacco, roll the cigarettes, and sell them on the floors during my daily laundry runs. Let that sink in for a minute: I was tearing out the pages of God's holy Word to roll cigarettes to sell to criminals.

✝

As I conducted my nightly cottage industry of rolling "holy smokes," my mind wandered to events in my past. I saw the broken relationship with my family, the dysfunction, and the bizarre childhood near drowning at the beach in particular. And siblings, whom I viewed not as friends or even family—just roommates who were dealt the same bad hand in life as I. The embers inside me burned hotter as I tore out pages of the Bible, finally realizing that my anger was directed at a God who, if He was real, had abandoned me altogether. And this joke of a book, given to me by a good-hearted security officer, was somehow supposed to lighten my load . . . ease my burdens. How could this book begin to touch the pain that I carried? How could its author, whoever that was, know where I'd been and the baggage I brought with me? How could my life turn out this way while a loving God ruled the universe?

With a clenched jaw, I kept tearing out pages, finding some deep satisfaction in knowing that these words would never be read by another human being, that they would evaporate into thin air to feed the addiction of some broken human being. God's words, gone up in smoke.

I asked myself in a wry way, *Doesn't this mean His Word returned void?* I was making a liar out of Him, so I thought. This was my retaliation, my revenge. So I sat alone in my cell, rolling smokes, defiling His Word . . . angrily shaking my fist at a God I did not know.

CHAPTER 6

DEEPER INTO SATANISM

*Do not deceive yourselves. If any of you think you are
wise by the standards of this age, you should become
"fools" so that you may become wise. For the wisdom of
this world is foolishness in God's sight. As it is written:
"He catches the wise in their craftiness"; and again, "The
Lord knows that the thoughts of the wise are futile."*

—1 CORINTHIANS 3:18–20

O n the day of release, my brother Dennis picked me up
from the Oklahoma County Jail and took me to get my
vehicle, a conversion van that had been in storage for the
past ten months. I spent most of the night at the car wash, cleaning
the van inside and out. This would be my new home.

The next few months, I lived in that van at various parking
lots around Oklahoma City. The nights were long and lonely, but
I was a free man, at least physically. Mentally, now that I was
out of jail, I kept thinking about the day I was walking from the
courtroom and hearing Chuck's jeering. I heard the remark of
the inmate I was handcuffed to: "If I were you, when I got outta
jail, I'd slit his throat, my man." I dreamed of silencing Chuck's
demeaning laugh forever.

Once again, as if I were crouched behind the wooden fence as in years past, I had to put the thought of hurting Chuck behind me. I thought of my three children, who meant everything to me. The simple pleasures of everyday life that aren't part of an enclosed six-by-ten-foot cell, with no windows, were enough to thwart any plan to go back "inside." The plan to hurt Chuck soon became a thing of the past.

I saw the sun and smelled the fresh air for the first time in ten months. I could sleep more soundly in my van than in a cell. Immediate danger was not something I had to live with 24/7 now. I could finally sleep with both eyes closed.

I began to reconnect with my children and look for carpentry work. I needed an income, a place to live, and some semblance of normalcy.

Don Nusbaum, the Christian friend who'd faithfully put money on my books in jail, found me after I was released. We'd worked together on projects before. He had just bid a job he needed help with and asked me to meet him at the job site. Nearly out of gas and hungry, I jumped at the opportunity.

Don walked me through the house and explained what needed to be done. I took the job and began work immediately. Don's timeline was short because the woman moving into the home was going through a divorce and wanted the renovation completed before she moved in.

Working in the kitchen, I met the owner, Maggie Rich, the following day. When I reflect on the divine appointments God put in my path, this one would prove to be monumental. Maggie and I seemed to click right away. I walked through the house with Maggie, explaining my background and offering ideas about how to proceed most efficiently. She was pleased.

Maggie became more involved as her move-in date

approached. She spent more time in the house, making design decisions, and we developed a rapport and began to talk about life. She was newly separated, and I was fresh out of jail. We were the walking wounded trying to recover from setbacks. Our initial friendship blossomed into a romance that led to a relationship that lasted twelve years.

Sadly, this relationship was founded on a lie. I led Maggie to believe I was a Christian early on in our friendship and really played the part to convince her. I knew she was a professed Christian and was leaning into that belief system, having just moved away from her husband in preparation for a divorce. I listened to some Christian music, gave the impression I was happy and upbeat, and projected the image of a Christ follower.

In my many hours around Christians and the churches I attended to wreak havoc, I learned a great deal about how to act. From my perspective, most Christians I encountered were just acting. They were simply going through the motions outwardly but secretly led another life. I didn't want to lead that type of life, other than to trick Christians into trusting me so I could lead them astray. In my mind, they were getting what they deserved: division, lack of spiritual power, and lack of true peace. The longer they suffered, the better. In their own lingo, they were reaping what they sowed.

I had in no way accepted Christ at this point, but looking back, my friendship with Maggie represented a positive change for me. Not that I was lying to a girl to get something from her—Satan had made me an expert at that. But this time I was searching, deeply troubled; what I wanted from this new friend was companionship. I was "double-minded" and "unstable" in all my ways, as James 1:8 says, but my motives were changing. I reached out in hopes of finding stability, some solid footing, friendship—and Maggie Rich, being the woman she was, took my hand.

Maggie, an interior decorator, stopped by the job one day and asked if I would accompany her on measuring and bidding a residential property. The huge old house was in a part of town she didn't feel comfortable being alone in. We even took her golden retriever, Ralph, with us for further support.

Obviously, this old stone house had been long neglected. As we drove up the long, dilapidated driveway, my spirit began to react. Something inside me prompted me that I'd been in this dark place before, in the spirit, and the heightened awareness that had been so acute in times past had my radar up again.

Maggie instructed me politely to observe and stay out of the way, as she only needed my help for measurements. The tenant would be available to answer any questions she might have. She walked along the east side of the house toward a rear entrance to meet the tenant while I followed close behind. The closer we moved to the rear of the house, the more agitated my spirit became.

A man appeared out of nowhere, and Maggie was startled at his sudden appearance. He was a thin man in his early forties. He had very pale skin, black hair, and a malnourished look to him. His face sunk in below his cheekbones, and it was evident his road traveled was a rough one. We've all seen those kinds. Usually it is a well-tanned person, unshaven, eyes that seem so deep . . . the homeless. But this guy was a hermit. Maggie and I were taken aback with his looks, and that contributed to both of us being on alert.

My senses were heightened due to the unusual way the man greeted us. With no forewarning, he just seemed to jump out at us. He didn't say a word but instead stared at us and waited for us to initiate conversation.

Despite her instructions for me to stay out of the way, I stepped between this stranger and Maggie and began sizing him up. Maggie's dog, Ralph, began to growl at the stranger and lean back on his hind legs.

The man and I noticed each other's scarred arms and glared at one another. A satanic staredown ensued. Instinctively I knew he, too, had crossed a line somewhere in his life and experienced the dark side of the supernatural. Self-mutilation can be a symptom of many things in the natural, but when spiritually driven, the scars all seem to take on the same appearance, size, and location on the body. It is hard to explain how one knows that, but it is a spiritual fact.

I was bigger physically, and in the unholy world in which we both operated, I also had more power. When I stepped between him and Maggie, I spoke quietly the native language we both knew well: a satanic language known as Enochian. I told him, "I will cut your heart out and eat it if I see you again!" I am not sure I would have. It was the past, surfacing to defend its territory: an ancient instinct finding expression in me at that moment.

He backed down, and we entered the house. Oddly, we never saw him again. I am quite certain the words I spoke to him caused him to leave.

Maggie and I walked through the foyer and noticed to our right a small room where the pale man had been sleeping. Cluttered and filthy, every inch of the room's walls was covered with Scripture verses written in different colors of ink. The writing was very small, allowing for thousands of verses to be penned. Just as I had memorized Scripture in jail, I surmised the man had done the same in this small room. To know an enemy, one needs to know his doctrine, what drives him, and his theology or philosophy. Learn it better than him, and there's a good chance you can capture his mind and control him.

Several Bibles in different translations and languages were strewn about. The windows were darkened by black paint. A small, black lamp sitting on an antique red oak nightstand lit the room. A tattered black throw rug partially covered a stained wood floor. I was on high alert as we moved further into the house.

Through a narrow hall we entered a large living area. To our left were two eight-foot-tall entry doors. To our right was a winding, three-story staircase, exposed by a thirty-foot ceiling in the room. The front doors were wedged shut by a full-size telephone pole (the type used along highways and in most backyards) that extended from the doors to the first step on the once elegant but now dilapidated staircase. Lack of electricity left us with only a little light from scattered windows. A thick layer of dust covered the floors and furniture. The house appeared to have been vacant for decades.

A door by the staircase led to a basement. Maggie opened the door and said, "There isn't enough money in this world to entice me to go down there." We didn't. She closed the door. Maggie went first up the staircase, with Ralph and me following close behind.

On the second level, Maggie entered a large bathroom and immediately noticed a hand-painted mural on the wall. This eye-catching piece of work had intricate colors, shapes, and loose outlines of faces. She was impressed enough to call me in to see it. When I walked in the room, I felt a current run up my spine. I recognized the satanic artwork at once. Maggie looked at me curiously as I studied the drawings. I noticed the artist's attention to demonic detail and then began to explain to Maggie the artist's themes and purpose. I would imagine that standing in a house that looked like something out of a Wes Craven film, then having your male friend break down the intricacies of demonic artwork, wouldn't put a girl at ease. Maggie looked at me a little wide-eyed, but to her credit, she soldiered on.

The rest of the house was equally dirty. We came to a place on the east side of the staircase we thought was an end, only to find a staircase to another level. Maggie looked at me and said, "Here we go."

I stepped backward. "No thanks, I'm done here. I'll meet you downstairs," I replied.

Just then, the hair on Ralph's back stood on end and he backed up, along with me. Ralph whined and was visibly shaken. I knew something was wrong, and the dog knew something was wrong, so with great apprehension, we watched Maggie march up the stairs and out of sight. It's my belief that Ralph's odd behavior was directly related to the dark spiritual presence on the property, because animals can be sensitive to paranormal and spiritual activities. He always seemed nervous around me.

You might wonder, why did I retreat in this situation? Why would a satanist be uncomfortable around my own people, so to speak? I was exhausted at this time. I'd reached a point where dealing with the dark side on this level had lost its luster. My body, mind, and spirit had been ravaged by my addiction to the macabre. But it was more than that: I saw something in that house. A scene flashed through my head that made me recoil from that room. I saw a little, blonde girl in a pale green dress being led up those stairs, and my spirit told me she was taken there for a sinister purpose. I didn't see the end result, but I knew she was there for a satanic ritual. This house had been a stronghold for evil. I knew something wicked had transpired here, and I wanted to get out.

After a few long moments, I heard Maggie gasp. She hurried down the stairs, her face ashen. Ralph barked and ran to her. I waited for her to regain her composure.

"You all right?" I asked. With her breathing labored, she nodded but didn't speak. Ralph sniffed all around her and whined.

Maggie caught her breath, then said, "I don't want to measure; in fact, I don't want anything to do with this project! Let's just go."

We rode in silence for a while, Maggie's eyes staring straight ahead until she finally broke the quiet. "What's going on in there, Mike?"

I dreaded my next words. "I'm sure it's a place where ritual killings happened . . . human sacrifice. I know there was a little girl sacrificed in that house."

The look of horror on her face made me wince.

We rode along for a bit. Then I said, "You saw something, didn't you?"

Maggie nodded. "When I got to the top of the stairs and walked in that room, I felt this heavy pressure on my chest; then all the air was sucked out of me. I couldn't breathe." I noticed her white-knuckling the wheel as she told the story. "Then, I had this—I don't know—vision, where, in a flash . . . I saw the whole floor plan in my head. I knew it was right too, without measuring, without drawing, no diagrams, nothing. Everything laid out like

I'd been in that house a hundred times." I looked away, knowing where the conversation was headed.

Maggie looked deep in thought and then said, "How do you know what happened in there—I mean, the little-girl thing you talked about? How do you know what that art meant? How would anyone know any of that?" Her voice broke.

I finally told her part of the truth. "I used to be a satanist."

If you're looking for a surefire way to make a woman go mute during a long car ride, tell her you've been a practicing satanist. It works every time.

We rode home in silence.

I carried on at the job site as if nothing had happened. Unfortunately, dark experiences like this were a normal part of the sad life I'd chosen, but Maggie's innocent world had just been rocked.

†|·

Strangely, we didn't speak again about this issue over the next month that I worked on Maggie's new home. I think she tried to bury the experience, and I wanted to appear as normal as I possibly could. Revisiting the event would only force me to reveal more about my strange past. Our conversations settled back into a comfortable place, and she seemed to relax around me again.

One secret that I was quite willing to keep from her was my living arrangement. The routine had worked like this: every day as I left her house, I would tell her I was going home, when in actuality, I was heading off to find a safe parking lot to sleep in my van for the night. Office buildings close to her house were a usual spot for me. On occasion, I would make it through the night without a security guard asking me to leave, and other nights I was not so lucky. On these sweltering August nights, falling asleep was a real chore. I remember waking up in a puddle of sweat on more than one occasion, and I often would succumb to opening the windows, spraying myself with mosquito repellent, and hoping I could cool off enough to sleep. I'd "made my bed" in life, all right, and it was on the floor of a dirty, used van.

Like the homeless guy that I was, I'd find a convenience store bathroom to clean up in before I went to work. Depressed, I ate sporadically, if at all; and life itself was a struggle. In a strange twist of common sense, I felt that depriving myself of a basic necessity gave me control over my flesh and made me more of an obedient vessel for evil to do its bidding through me. In my opinion, on either side of the fence of good or evil, self-control produced leaders.

I started a second job for a friend who was kind enough to let me stay at the house I was working on, which happened to be only a few miles from Maggie's place. My friendship with her blossomed into a dating relationship, and although I had finished her remodel project, we began to see each other regularly outside the original homeowner/contractor relationship. I was able to see my kids on weekends, and I began to find steady work. Life started to smooth out a little, in no small measure because of Maggie. I had a general direction, I was working regularly, I was in a relationship, and I began to feel much better about my life.

Well, you know what they say about feelings: don't trust them. Things were about to get a whole lot worse.

Being the creative person she was, Maggie came up with a business idea that included me. She proposed that since she was around the real estate market, she could purchase houses at a low price, I could repair them, she would decorate them, and then we'd sell them for a nice profit. In the real estate world, this process is called "flipping houses."

Her business proposal seemed like a good fit. I would have a steady client, with a chance to get ahead. She would have someone she could trust on the job and could make a good income in the process. She had the financial credit. I had the experience to go into a house, estimate costs, and complete the project with little or no outside help. After nine months, we incorporated.

The business arrangement with Maggie was short-lived, as she took on a business partner with whom I didn't get along. After a couple of small project houses, I walked away from the business partnership and never looked back. My mind was on greater things. Consumed with thoughts of separation from ordinary life, I soon made isolation my best friend.

✝

Before I'd gone to jail, I'd installed entry doors for a local lumber company. After Maggie and I started flipping houses, I contacted a gentleman who owned a door manufacturing facility in Canada and started installing doors for him nationwide.

Working solo, I installed doors in twenty states until I developed a network of subcontractors. With interest rates at next to nothing, home building exploded, and so did my business. About five years into the operation, I had fourteen people working in my central offices and about five hundred contractors nationwide.

Our company averaged about one thousand service calls a month and grossed close to three million dollars that fifth year. This was quite a leap from sleeping in a van.

Yet, it seems I had little tolerance for prosperity. I was on the road for months at a time; the travel began to take its toll, and Satan began to reassert his evil presence into my life. My life is a prime example of the fact that Satan loves isolation, when people are disconnected and unaccountable. He knows that with believers, there is strength in numbers. Satan is no fool—he attacks where he is strongest and we're most vulnerable.

So, barreling down that old, gray snake all alone, my depression returned, my anxiety increased, and my thoughts became more and more unstable. With the depression and uncontrolled thought life, I'd given the adversary a direct path into my mind. I am both surprised and truly thankful that during this time, I didn't kill myself or someone else.

Constantly bombarded with thoughts so bizarre and evil that I found myself shaking my head to try to get them out, my mind became a depository of satanic thoughts and vile imagery. I'd see a man step off a curb, a scene would flash in my head of him lying lifeless under my wheels, and I would have to physically stop myself from running over him. I envisioned myself at a local gun range, target practicing, then opening fire on the unsuspecting patrons as they concentrated on their efforts. Many times I saw myself falling off ladders, stepping off a cliff, falling from a tall building, and in similar instances where I was severely hurt or killed. I would perhaps be working in my shop, cutting a piece of wood on my table saw, and would have a vision of my arm being sawed off and blood covering the walls and ceiling. My mind was a sewer of disjointed, detached, and perverted thoughts.

I kept a 9mm Glock in the truck at all times. I was deadly accurate with it though I seldom practiced. I'd go to a gun range on rare occasions and would bury every shot inside the target no more than two inches from the center at long distance. Then I'd bring the targets to Maggie's home and tape them to a window where the sun could shine through to show how accurate I was. And perhaps to passively show what a mistake it would be for anyone to cross me.

Maggie and I got along well for the most part during this period of life, until she began to develop new friends I didn't like and jealousy began to rear its ugly head. She spent a lot of time with Art, a single personal trainer and martial arts teacher. When I went out of town, he and Maggie would meet for lunch dressed in their "kung fu jammies" and do their martial arts training a couple times a week. You can imagine how I reacted when she lit up whenever Art's name was mentioned. She would rattle off his laundry list of accomplishments: a master's degree, an eighth-degree black belt, a chaplain, and the perfect gentleman.

It didn't end there. Maggie often took her laptop to work at a nearby coffee shop where men seemed to orbit around her. She was the only woman in a roomful of men. "Oh, we're just talking shop, honey," she'd tell me. "They're all in the real estate industry." I was less than convinced.

Once when I was leaving for an out-of-town trip, I kissed Maggie good-bye and she told me she had errands to run. Heading toward the highway out of town, I felt the urge to swing by the coffee shop. When I walked in, her back was to me and she was chattering away at a table with her male friends.

"Hi, there," I said. Maggie jumped, and as I sat down, the man she was talking with scurried away. I stared at her for a few long seconds and could sense her anxiety. Finally, I leaned over the table and said quietly, "You won't be having coffee here tomorrow; I can guarantee that. This place will burn tonight."

Maggie looked dumbstruck. I left.

✝

I was somewhere in the middle of Indiana the next day when Maggie called, asking me where I was. She was on speakerphone, and I figured her friend Art was listening to our conversation. I told her, but she didn't believe me. I gave her a local number she could call to verify where I was. She called me back on the landline and was shocked I wasn't in town.

The coffee shop had caught fire the previous night and was closed when she went there the next morning. I didn't start the fire, but I had seen a vision about it. I knew it was going to burn, and I knew why: an insurance scam by the owner. Satan had allowed me to take credit for this to scare Maggie even more. Satan had me believing I could accomplish anything I wanted in the spirit of his dark power if I had cause. The only other action needed from me was to summon the spirits necessary and wait in faith for the resulting deed to transpire.

I crisscrossed the country, checking on jobs, completing work, and seeing new clients. I would often travel from one state to the next, remembering little of how I got there. On my long trips to Albuquerque, I stared out the window at the open desert and felt a surge in my spirit. In the seclusion and isolation, I sensed a new energy growing as darkness continued to fill me. Since I was an open vessel for satanic forces, ever-increasing darkness continued to flow in. The road became my new addiction, and the path I traveled was destruction.

The minute I got home, I couldn't wait to leave on another business trip. Every trip, I felt more empowered by Satan. Like any addict, I'd become a master at hiding my activities, a real deceiver.

I drove on automatic pilot across the country. The part of me that could have marveled at the natural beauty and God's brilliant design was held captive by Satan. I do not remember the waving wheat in Oklahoma, the sunflowers in Kansas, or the bluebonnets in Texas. I didn't see the massive breadth of the Mississippi River. The lapping waves of the Gulf of Mexico landing on its sugar-white shores went unheard. The Rocky Mountains were a nuisance to cross. New England was a blur. The tall pines in the South just shaded the highway. I am sure the desert cactus bloomed, but I didn't see it. All I could see was the growing dark power inside me.

✝

My firm, Doorways USA, began dealing with a company on the West Coast. Most of the business we had at this time was primarily east of New Mexico. But with the new business relationship, I received an order in Utah and had no one available nearby to take care of the claim. I headed there to handle it personally.

Barreling west on I-40, I was looking for a place to eat after a hard day's driving when I spilled coffee on my shirt. I pulled onto Highway 666 (yes, there is a Highway 666, and it is where

I pulled off) and into a local Walmart to purchase some stain remover. Searching a shelf, I heard a voice behind me say, "Satan wants you back." I turned to see a lady with long, black hair walking by. I stared at her back for a moment; then she turned and offered up a sly smile. Wanted me back? I'd never really left. Everybody hates those who sit on the fence, and I guess Satan was no exception; I had to be firm in my resolve.

After driving most of the night with that strange encounter on my mind, I pulled into Salt Lake City, Utah, the next morning and found the house of my customer, Sue. I pulled into her driveway and found her working in her yard. I introduced myself and began to analyze her door situation. The problem was an installation issue, so the manufacturer wasn't on the hook; the owner was. But I had traveled a very long way and had the energy and time to make the corrections, so I did.

The reinstall of the unit took about four hours. During the process, Sue sat on a staircase and talked with me. She was appreciative and understood I was doing this as a goodwill effort to help her out.

In her midthirties, Sue was both attractive and divorced. We talked about many things, including her Mormon faith. We discussed the rules and doctrines the Mormons lived under and talked about Joseph Smith and the history of the church and its commitment to family. I found it very interesting. I had spoken to Mormons in the past, but the conversations were shallow and short.

Sue was intrigued with the spiritual energy I had, an intensity she found attractive. I sensed a lustful spirit and knew all I had to do was nudge her to the edge, and Satan would do the rest. She invited me to stay for dinner.

We continued our conversation over dinner, where I turned the conversation to sex. She said it was forbidden outside of marriage and that if she succumbed, she wouldn't be allowed to walk into the temple. She would be excluded from the holy place. After a few hours, I guess she wasn't going to the holy place. When I was set to leave her house, she really wanted to go with me; it didn't matter where, just anywhere away from Utah and the drudgery of her life.

With jobs to tend to and a girlfriend waiting back home, her coming with me was not an option. I headed back east to complete a few jobs before I turned south to Louisiana and then east to Florida. A couple of weeks later on the same trip, I called Sue. She was happy I called and asked where I was. When I mentioned I was on the way to Florida, she said she had always wanted to go there. I offered to fly her down if she could manage a babysitter. She said she could, and I made the arrangements.

Two days later we were sharing some time in Florida. I asked her how she felt.

"About what?" she asked coyly.

"About sleeping with Satan," I replied, my eyes boring into hers. I watched the color drain from her face as she lay back slowly on her pillow, wondering how to take that comment.

"Yeah, right," she finally said, studying me to see what my response would be.

I got out of bed to use the restroom and never said a word. Sue and I never discussed the matter again. You think an STD is bad; try sleeping with somebody who's walking with the devil—a Satanically Transmitted Disease.

✝️

The success of my business allowed me to relax a little and begin to look for things to fill my time on the road when I wasn't fixing doors, training new contractors, or in meetings with clients. Being able to downshift can be a good thing, but the way I was wired, money and idle time were the twin evils that allowed me to fuel my addictions. And the bright neon lights of the casinos beckoned.

About twice a week, I'd drop as much as ten thousand dollars at a blackjack table. Sometimes I won, and won big, but most of the winnings went back into a machine or a table, and the futile cycle continued. I loved the adrenaline, craved the action, and would play nonstop through the night, riding the moment, in touch with nothing but my own cravings for more action, more stimulus, a slave to self, where no peace was to be found.

Looking back, the gambling addiction was one that was handed down from my parents. My siblings and I recall the six-hundred-mile round-trip we would take every two weeks from our California home to Las Vegas. Five children under the age of fifteen would sleep in an uninsulated and non-air-conditioned van in the desert heat for the weekend. We children waited in the heat for two days until our parents ran out of either money or time, or both. We always hoped they'd won so we could eat on the five-hour trip home. If our parents lost, we waited to eat until we got home; and by the time that happened, we were too tired to eat.

My parents were addicted to the casinos, and it is a problem that my siblings and I have dealt with. I never considered myself to have an addictive personality. My belief is that the further I delved in the satanic and dark side, the more addictive my personality became.

My addiction to trying to mislead Christians seemed to pick up steam on the road as well. The farther I was away from home, the more my activities turned dark in nature. My great entertainment on the road came on Wednesday nights and Sundays. I would go into churches, find a couple of weak believers (which was usually easy), and try to undermine their faith. With men, I tried to manipulate Scripture. With women, the goal was seduction.

I'd go to a service after the praise and worship was finished, because I couldn't stand to be in the company of believers praising God. I'd listen to the message, then stick around in the foyer afterward and chat up the members. I'd sit around drinking coffee, and somebody would invite me to coffee or lunch. I'd try to get people one-on-one. I'd ask them what they thought about Scripture or the Word of God. It was astonishing how little most churchgoing people actually knew about the God they claimed to serve.

These conversations allowed me to test the water and measure the depth of believers' faith—it was usually shallow. And this gave me opportunity to penetrate their weak spiritual defenses. I would twist Scripture and plant seeds of doubt in their minds. Or take a well-known Bible verse and start down the path of "Does it really mean that?" New Testament verses would roll off my tongue, and at first blush, I seemed like a member of the family, mixing easily with the other believers. Sadly, most were unaware of my motives.

Out on the road alone, my sinister activities continued, and over time my mental instability increased. Plagued with depression, anger, and frustration, I had renewed my allegiance to Satan and began to serve him solely.

The further I went down this demonic highway, the quicker I stopped straddling the fence and served him whom I knew best. In 1 Kings 18:21, Elijah tells the people there: "How long will you waver between two opinions? If the LORD is God, follow him; but if Baal is God, follow him." The problem I had was that I didn't really know whom to serve, so when the going got tough, I went back to what I knew: Satan.

While traveling around the country, I also found it amusing to buy and distribute satanic bibles to unsuspecting victims. I would throw paperbacks in the bushes in and around Christian schoolyards and under pews in churches. I would put them anywhere I could in the hopes that someone would pick one up and read it. Again, sowing seeds was part of Satan's plan in my life. Perhaps one out of ten persons might become involved in the activities in the book. The power of the dark side would then lure them in.

I spent the next year or so on the road, working my business. I had two cell phones, a laptop in my truck with a GPS and wireless Internet connection, and all the tools at my fingertips to help run the business from anywhere. I used an American Express card for the twenty thousand dollars or so I spent a month for expenses, toys, and whatever I wanted. The more my CFO would tell me to curb the expenses, the more I spent. Years later, he would get the opportunity to "tell me so."

✝

During this time, Maggie read several books on the subject of psychology, deliverance, religion, spiritual warfare, God, the devil, demons, and whatever other book she could get her hands on to try to figure out what was going on with me. Determined to get help for me, she spoke to physicians the world over. She talked to a doctor in Bangladesh and some in other countries, and her takeaway was that the problem was spiritual.

She insisted I start going to a nearby psychologist named Ann. I went to her for over a year, and she said I had PTSD (post-traumatic stress disorder), brought on by childhood experiences (and the overdose I practically died from) as well as a ton of spiritual baggage I had been carrying with me. Ann told me that I needed to find the God I was looking so hard for. Both she and Maggie said they had never seen such a quest for spiritual truth. I knocked, and the doors just wouldn't open. I asked and did not receive. I sought and could not find.

Since childhood I have had blackouts, time lapses, periods of a particular day or event that I flat-out don't remember. As a young adult, I saw doctors who attempted to diagnose the issue. The doctors had no clue other than to say the problems could be caused by one of several injuries I had had up to this point in my life: a near drowning when I was six, the overdose when I was nineteen, and the fall from the attic when I was twenty that put me in the hospital.

I went to several shrinks during my younger years. Diagnoses would tend to be one of about thirty items in the DSM-IV (clinical diagnosis guideline book). The more I went, the more I enjoyed memorizing sections of the DSM-IV and challenging the doctors. As long as someone was paying for it, I didn't care what they told me; it was a form of entertainment for me.

These episodes of lapsed consciousness became more frequent the deeper I got into satanism and routinely happened after rituals. In the satanic events, these lapses occurred quite often; especially after summons for help (I would ask spirits to help in situations where I felt overloaded in the flesh).

The blackouts became more pervasive, as did my visits with the dark side. On weekends and evenings, I often went to Barnes & Noble with Maggie. She loved reading, getting a coffee, and relaxing. I would drift into the store and would forage the New Age section. I didn't purchase as much as I simply soaked up the pages of hundreds of books on religion, Wicca, satanism, the occult, black magic, psychology, and philosophy. I had to read quickly, hide what I was reading behind magazine covers, or go into the restroom to read. If Maggie had caught me opening those books or even venturing into the New Age section, she would have flipped out and realized I was more lost than she could have ever imagined.

CHAPTER 7

BLACK SHADOWS

This is how you can recognize the Spirit of God: Every spirit that acknowledges that Jesus Christ has come in the flesh is from God, but every spirit that does not acknowledge Jesus is not from God. This is the spirit of the antichrist, which you have heard is coming and even now is already in the world.

—1 JOHN 4:2–3

Fall was turning the oak leaves, and between business road trips, I was remodeling a new home Maggie and I bought. The construction process took nearly three years. I was living there, and Maggie and her three children were living in her home. The plan was for the four of them to move in and join me when this house was finished.

The house was empty other than the supplies, lumber, and tools strewn about, and a mattress I slept on. All of my personal belongings, furniture, and keepsakes were stowed in the garage. One evening, I was working in the new addition of my house: painting, texturing, and tiling. About 6 p.m. I heard a knock on the door. I made my way to the front door and found no one there.

I walked back to the new bedroom and continued plastering the walls. Beyond the four patio doors in the backyard, I observed the beauty of two landscaped acres. The leaves were falling from the hundreds of trees that encompassed the acreage. As the sun began to set, the brisk air blew through an open window.

Another noise came from the front of the house. Suddenly, I heard the alarm beep that sounds when a door is opened. Someone must've come inside. I yelled, "I'm back here" to whoever entered, believing it was either Maggie or one of my kids checking in to see the progress. After a few minutes with no response, I went out to the main living area and found no one. One of the patio doors appeared to have blown open, so I closed and locked it. I walked back down the forty-foot hallway to get back to work.

I became sensitive in the spirit. I was in a state of heightened awareness and acutely in tune to spiritual forces around me, a sort of knowledge of the spiritual realm. This usually manifested in a sickening feeling in my stomach, which knotted up. A heaviness came over me and typically would send me into the fight-or-flight mode. For instance, it would be similar to what a woman might feel when walking down a dark street to get to her car and instinctively knowing there is someone behind her. When she turns, there is a man quickly approaching whom she did not notice before. Or there could be a case where a man is out hunting in dense woods and hears the crackling of dry brush being crushed under a heavy foot close behind him. Well, amplify this feeling tenfold while knowing someone else is in a dark room with you, but that someone isn't flesh and blood. That someone is a spirit.

How do I know this? I experienced it in the conjuring of spirits in my satanic practices. I saw things that most probably don't.

But most people have had that feeling and can't pin down what it is. Most have been scared to death of something they could not see. Most have had times when they were very frightened in the dark of night at perhaps a noise that was created by no obvious means. Many have had ghost stories told to them that gave them goose bumps . . . that is the feeling I am referring to.

I continued painting the walls and ceilings. As the second coat was drying, I hopped into the shower to set the marble tile. I arranged my tasks around drying times and jumped from job to job so that every minute was efficient. I continued in a methodical and persistent pace without the waste of time. I analyzed every step and proceeded in an effective manner. This was the way it had to be. I liked that no one was around, and I was undisturbed in purpose. The hours were passing quickly.

It was 11:30 p.m., and I had only a couple of hours of work to go. The mattress on the floor seemed to be my worst enemy. My thought was that if I didn't have to sleep, I would get so much more done. I returned to painting the final coat on a bedroom wall. I felt a presence and instinctively turned to look outside . . . a dark body flashed across the back lawn silently. I knew at once that I was being watched.

In the dark recesses of the backyard, I tried to stalk whatever was trying to observe me. I felt in my spirit a presence that meant to harm me. I sensed an uninvited guest both powerful and alluring. The crushing weight I felt in my spirit, a heightened nervousness and agitation, the heaviness, the hair raising on the back of my neck, all told me I'd been here before, in this situation. The presence of evil in the supernatural had become natural for me. It was familiar. Nothing appeared in the surrounding area, and I returned through the open door and continued to work.

The night air was cold, and inside a fire lit the fireplace to warm the room and help dry the newly painted walls. I locked the doors and wanted to return to work but was exhausted. I sat on the floor and eventually gave in to my mattress and sleeping bag.

The busyness I lived daily helped me become numb to the world. My four hours of sleep per night, which I had been used to for nearly twenty years, interfered with the projects I'd lined up. At the end of each workday, I collapsed in exhaustion at 1 a.m. I awoke between 4:30 and 5 a.m. and started another day. There were not enough hours in the day to complete the tasks I assigned myself. I worked feverishly and constantly day after day. The physical labor was a way to work off anxiety. It was also a way to keep from facing the mountain that lay ahead of me: the demise of my business, personal financial obliteration, my wrecked relationship with Maggie, and strained relationships with everyone I knew. Working nonstop was my way of going endlessly around the mountain instead of climbing and conquering it.

To break the monotony of inside tasks, the next day, my efforts were concentrated in the yard, raking up leaves and cleaning up. As I was working, a man in his midforties walked by with a toddler and a young boy. The man introduced himself as one of my new neighbors. Doug said he walked by every day and enjoyed seeing the improvements I was making to the property and the neighborhood. He said he was a Christian and asked me if I was. I told him no. He also mentioned the rigorous hours I worked and told me that every time he and his wife, Jill, drove by, I was diligently working. Doug was bold in asking me what I thought I was hiding from.

Doug made a statement that I didn't want to consider: "It took more effort, it seemed, to face the giant as David did Goliath than to run from him as everyone else did." I told him that I enjoyed working and I never feared giants . . . I joined them; I embraced my fears. He asked if I had a family, and to shut down the conversation I told him I had to get back to work. I knew he had unanswered questions, but I was on a schedule and wasn't in the mood to share my personal life with him.

Every day Doug walked by the house. If I was outside, he would say hello and continue his walk with his children.

About the third week of being off the road, it was time for me to make another business trip. I left Oklahoma on a trip through Missouri, Texas, Louisiana, and Mississippi, and I would get back home a week later. I was north of Joplin, Missouri, when my truck started having engine problems. I pulled into a truck stop to determine what was going on. Obviously the truck would need a stop in a shop to be fixed. It appeared certain that several of my fuel injectors had quit working in the engine. The engine was losing power and running rough.

For the past several months, I had been in contact with one of Maggie's longtime friends, Cathy. We had exchanged information when I met Cathy and her husband, Mark, at a large birthday party of a friend of Maggie's. When we spoke on the phone, the main topic of conversation was God. She professed to be a Christian, but I could sense that she was not; her actions told me a different story. Our talks centered on spiritual beliefs and doctrines, and we appeared to have a tie in the spirit and felt close to one another even though we hadn't known each other long. Except for the one face-to-face meeting, we only spoke via phone, usually weekly. Cathy and Mark were having marital issues that had been troubling them for years. They were still living in the same house but carrying on separate lives.

I was on the phone with Cathy when I drove into the truck stop. As we talked, a heaviness and sense of loss of control came over me. We were talking about deep spiritual concerns. I felt as if something or someone was trying to take over my body. My phone indicated I had another call, and when I switched calls, it was Maggie. I explained my feelings of spiritual darkness to Maggie. She said that since I happened to be near Cathy's hometown, I should take the truck to a Ford dealer near Cathy, go to her house, and chill; it would all be okay. I don't think Cathy told Maggie we had been in touch by phone lately, and I didn't volunteer the information to her.

Maggie could tell from my voice that I was getting agitated and starting to get spiritually disturbed. Since telling Maggie of my past, she had begun to pick up when I was sensitive, little nuances that would at times grow into what seemed to her, as she shared with me, straight-out possession. It would typically begin with becoming agitated over the simplest thing and turn to trembling of hands and then a full-blown anger that erupted. Maggie told me that my eyes would dilate like a snake's eyes, and the whites of my eyes would turn reddish in color. Sonnae Albert, the prophetic woman of God I mentioned earlier, said she had witnessed this as well. Many others claim to have seen the anomaly happen to me.

I was still deep in the satanic, and although I had moments of clarity, Satan would lull his way into my life at times to complete assignments, and then I would fade back into some form of normalcy. A heightened sense of awareness engulfed my spirit, and I blacked out mentally and sometimes physically—as though my mind had been made suddenly clearer by separating from my body, an eventual eruption of controlling spirits in me. The blackouts, I believe, were a built-in circuit breaker and relay that directed all my energy to a central purpose for an optimal result: spiritual control for some spiritual purpose.

I found myself driving south on the highway toward Cathy's house. My left arm had a deep gash about five inches long on it. At a roadside store I stopped to buy butterfly bandages to close the wound. A few miles down this very same road was a dealership, where I took my truck to get repaired. I called Cathy and asked her to pick me up. She had taken the day off after being prompted by Maggie that I was in serious need of prayer and help. As soon as we got to her house, we continued our discussion on spiritual matters. I discussed the evil one and told her how intertwined I had been with him over the years.

Her husband was at work. As we were discussing the past and present evil in my life, Cathy mentioned that, while she wasn't sure of her own faith, she had friends who were Christians who might be able to offer me relief. She asked if I would be interested in meeting with them.

She invited her Christian friends over for a discussion and some prayer. I don't remember them or what went on. Most often when I found myself in a deliverance setting or when I partook in a spiritual battle, I would fade in the flesh, enter into the spirit, and lose my memory of the event.

Time passed. It was evening when they left, and I watched TV while Cathy did a few home chores, ran some errands, and took care of other normal family things until bedtime. Mark came home, and we chatted some before he went to bed.

I fell asleep on the couch in the living room. About 3 a.m. I was awakened by someone tucking a blanket around me. I opened my eyes to see Cathy dressed in white lingerie, with a sensual look on her face. She also had her hand under the blanket, caressing me. She joined me on the couch, and we slept together, her husband just a few yards away. At the time, it mattered little to me that her husband was just separated from us by a single door. It didn't appear to bother Cathy either.

After thirty minutes or so, I got up to use the restroom, and when I came out, she was on the phone talking softly with someone with a sly smile on her face.

I thought it was weird that she was on the phone at this hour and asked her who it was. She told me it was Maggie and was in the process of telling her what had just happened. She had an evil look on her face that turned to a smile from time to time. When I asked her what the heck she was doing, she told me she wanted Maggie to know. Cathy was definitely making a statement, and I believed she not only planned this event but had long-standing issues with Maggie.

I became angry with Cathy for her behavior. At 6 a.m. I went for a walk. I had nowhere to go since my truck was in the shop, and I was on foot. I must have walked for miles when I noticed a car following me. Cathy pulled over and asked me to get in the car and go back home. We drove back to her house, where I stayed for the next few days until my truck was repaired. Cathy and I had several more sessions during that time. When repairs on my truck were complete, Cathy took me to pick up my truck.

✝

When I arrived home a week later, I didn't expect the response I got. Maggie welcomed me home, and little was said.

Both Maggie and I continued on that day and the rest of the week in as normal a fashion as we could with what had happened between me and her now ex-friend. This was just one more relationship of hers that I entered into and ended up ruining. During our years together, a variety of relationships between Maggie and her friends and family were taxed due to the darkness in my life. Satan did everything in his power to use me to destroy the lives I touched.

The day after I arrived home from my trip, I traveled thirty miles north of Maggie's house to work on the Oak Creek house that we were building. As I walked up the sidewalk to the front of the house, I noticed six dead crows lined up in front of the door. It was a sign of some kind, and I wondered who would do this. I also wondered why they did it. I threw the birds in the trash and entered the house. As soon as I stepped in, I felt an intense urge to contact my spirit guide.

I walked through the house to make sure everything was okay and that no unwanted physical or spiritual guests were there. I turned on lights, powered up the air compressor, and prepared for an evening and night of work. At this time, I had a full-size bed in the TV room and occasionally would rest some. This was the first place I headed. When I walked in the room, I lay on the bed and concentrated as I channeled and spiritually left the room.

The further I drifted into the spirit realm, the more intense and focused I became. The natural world faded and the spiritual world came to reality. Black shadows (evil spirits) invaded the room and the house, touching everything in sight. They bounced around in a hurried fashion as if on a mission long delayed. Since I was already consumed with darkness, they moved past me as they were released to carry out the vision implanted in them. Their motion was constant, unwavering, and uninterrupted.

As the dark forces were invading, they did not notice the one who had ushered them in: me. They were free at this moment in time to unleash that which was in them, which was pure evil and darkness; like a male dog marking its territory, they were claiming this space as theirs. They were all consuming, and no space was untouched. The rooms were filled with despair and a sense of loss; a complete void of love, affection, and light.

A door opened, and someone entered the house. I felt the spirit of my daughter Kristin. Her breath left her body as she gasped for air. I heard her prayers and voice as she called to me. I was nowhere near, and could not react to her attempt to bring me back to a place of choice and rational thought. But because I loved her and was trying to protect her, I became torn in the spirit. The spiritual war was so great that the longer she stayed, the closer to death I came. The lack of light and love quickly forced my baby girl outside and away from the house. She left, and moments later, as my spirit fell back into my body, I awoke and scanned the room.

On the concrete floor, a pentagram was drawn with a magic marker. On each of the points were lit votive candles. Drops of dried blood were inside the star, and a knife was cautiously placed outside the circle that encompassed it. Heavy drops of blood led from the makeshift altar to the bed were I lay. The blue sheets were moist with the blood that flowed from gashes on my body.

I slowly rose from bed and staggered into the living room. I walked the floors of the house in a dazed state. It was about 9 p.m., and I went into the backyard to get some air. I sat on a brick wall and tried to gather my thoughts. My body was weak, and it was hard for me to lift my head. Both my arms hung to my side and felt as if heavy weights were attached to them. When I got up to walk, it taxed my strength to make my way to my pickup truck to leave.

I slept in my truck in a nearby shopping center parking lot. I awoke the next morning to a burning pain from the cuts that were inflicted upon me only hours earlier. As I glanced at the cuts on my arm and looked at my bloodstained shirt that indicated cuts on my stomach, I passively thought of what remodel work I had planned to do that day and calmly cleaned up the mess.

I ventured back to the house to work on finishing my remodeling. I cleaned up the ritual site. The day was like most others, filled with hard physical labor and an attempt to avoid closeness with anyone. The hours of each day were full of work, and the nights were full of terror. I would wake up frequently during each night in a heavy sweat. Loud chanting, footsteps on the floor, or the sensation of someone close enough to me that I felt breath in my face, alerted me and pulled me from my slumber. Each day that passed became more conflicted between the natural world and the spirit realm. The times in which the nights were full of the spirit and the days full of the natural were becoming a thing of the past. The spiritual side of my life was taking over and was now dominant twenty-four hours a day.

The result was heightening chaos, loss of sleep and rest, and diminished mental comprehension and awareness. I was losing my mind, it seemed, in stages. My heart and mind were inching toward a place of no return regarding an eternal choice of life and death—seared, separated.

My phone rang, and it was my daughter Kristin, who said

without pause, "Dad, I don't even know what to say, but what I saw yesterday I will never forget. What in God's earth are you really into? I can't help you, Dad, but God can! I have turned you over to God. But I am not going to quit; I am going to find help. Dad, I pray for you constantly! I believe God will deliver you from the hell you are in. Do you need medical help, Dad? . . . I saw the blood."

"No, I am okay, Krissy. I don't need medical help. I don't remember much of yesterday. Yeah, things are getting worse. It will end soon, I promise."

Kristin blurted back, "Dad, you better reach out. And *now*! I'm going to talk with my pastor—anyone—but I am not going to let Satan take you out! This has gone on way too long! Satan, be gone! Leave my dad alone!"

I didn't have time to respond before she angrily hung up the phone. I didn't try to call her back but returned to work, an irrational response to the irrational life I lived.

The day passed quickly with my busy workload, and evening was near. The next day another road trip was scheduled. That night, my friend David was coming to help me with painting the living room and hall. I would concentrate on prepping the concrete floors so I could install wood floors when I returned from this business trip.

The day was growing long, and David finally showed up. He began painting in the hall as I continued working on the floor in the den. I got a call from Maggie asking if I would be coming by her house before I left town. I checked the time, saw it was nearly 9 p.m., and told David I was going to see Maggie and her kids. I told him I would be back in the morning before I left town and asked him to lock up when he was finished.

At Maggie's house we talked briefly about the remodel progress, and after we chatted with the kids awhile, everyone went to
sleep.

I awoke early the next day. Maggie and I had coffee and
enjoyed early morning conversation, breakfast, and our usual
good-byes before I went to my house to pick up the trailer and
tools I needed for another journey on the road.

I arrived at the Oak Creek house about 8 a.m. and noticed
that the overhead garage door was open. I figured that David was
still there but did not see his truck. The entry door to the house
from the garage was also open. I walked into the kitchen and
looked through the living area to the hall where David had been
working and noticed spilled paint and a paint roller on the floor.
The ladder was lying on its side. His shoeprints were on the floor
where he had walked through the paint on his way to leave the
house. It appeared he left in a hurry.

The appearance of the house concerned me. I was hopeful
David hadn't fallen and hurt himself. With the doors left open
and the house a mess, I figured something drastic had happened.
I immediately called David to see if he was okay. He didn't answer
his cell phone. I then called his house phone and was relieved to
hear his voice.

David told me he had decided to work into the morning.
He said he heard some strange noises outside and went out to
investigate. He had a strange feeling when he went back into the
house. He got back on the ladder. When he was painting the cor-
ners of the wall and ceiling in the living room, he heard someone
walking down the hall. In fact, it sounded as if many people were
coming his way. He also heard voices with the footsteps, and they
were deep voices, chanting in a strange language.

David said he was so frightened that he dropped his brush, jumped off the ladder, knocking it over, spilled the paint, and accidentally ran through it as he bolted out the door. He jumped in his truck, hurried away from the house, and went home. When he got home, he told his wife, and they prayed about it. I never heard any more about the night David had the encounter. It became an out-of-sight, out-of-mind memory and event.

I cleaned up the paint mess and gathered my tools, cleaned the trailer, and loaded for the trip. Within an hour I had readied the truck and trailer. I left the house for a short trip to work in Kansas City, go by a client's door factory to pick up parts, and come back home. The trip would only take three days, and then I would be back to finish the house and move in.

After I returned from my trip, I finished installing the floors at Oak Creek and completed the other projects necessary to move in. It took me ten days. In the following two weeks, Maggie and I moved into our newly remodeled home. We quickly filled the house with the possessions from our previous homes. Her three children liked their new home, the great backyard, and the extra room the larger house provided. All seemed well. A twelve-hundred-square-foot building fit nicely in the landscaped backyard and provided both Maggie and me with nicely remodeled office space. She had her office for residential interior design work, and it gave her a quiet retreat. Our offices had different entrances, and I generally would use this home office instead of my company's central office. It was a quieter and more relaxed setting.

I also had built a shop on the south side of my office that I used for working on my motorcycles. I had a couple of older Harleys I enjoyed toying with. The room had windows and a heat-and-air unit that kept the area pleasant year-round. I retreated regularly there to work on my mechanical projects and hobbies.

Daily life issues, such as relationships, business, earning a living, house and grounds maintenance, kids, and our normal daily routine, kept me busy twenty hours per day. I took no time for rest, recreation, exercise, healthy contemplation, or any positive activity to restore and keep my mind, emotions, and body in a healthy state. In all my years, I had never done this. I worked all the time to avoid thinking about the value of my life. I was afraid I might discover that feeling of meaninglessness. My work was my narcotic, my drug of choice—but it was a legit, moral escape from oblivion. A part of me still wanted to live a socially acceptable life, and no matter how much I worked, I figured no one would judge me a bad man for my workaholism.

✝

In 2003, Maggie and I had known each other six years and had lived in the Oak Creek house right at two years. Daily routine and busy schedules filled our days. As stressors increased in our relationship and in our lives, Maggie questioned my mental health because of all the spiritual trash she had personally witnessed, and she insisted I seek counseling again. She even told me she would pay for the counseling sessions. I tried to convince her that I was still hanging with my friend Bob Sanders some and thought that was all the help I needed. She countered that I needed much more time "in session" than the time I spent with him.

I was referred to a local female psychologist, Dr. Kelly Winters. I went one day a week for the next year. I didn't trust the mental health system, or the person I was seeing.

After six months of seeing Dr. Winters, I started to like her just as a person and would use our chats more as a time to converse. She had, however, diagnosed me with PTSD and explained the condition and ways to handle situations that may lead to manifestations of the symptoms. Symptoms generally didn't expose themselves unless I was in a situation that I perceived as harmful or where I felt I was in imminent danger.

Symptoms would range from extreme anxiety to physical violence. Often, I would exhibit a variety of undesirable behaviors in very stressful situations. The most pronounced situations were doctor and dental office visits. Combative or argumentative conversations were ripe for symptoms to pop up. The worst-case scenario would be prior to and after anesthesia was given to me in a surgery setting. And my biggest fear was lying down asleep, or perhaps drugged before a surgery, or incapacitated in any way on my back, and having people stand over me. I absolutely would come unglued. I had two knee surgeries and a couple surgeries on my nose (to correct damage from being broken a few times) during this period that put me in a place that was traumatic for me. Looking back, it was always a position over which I had no control and was usually a place where I was physically in a prone position. Something about lying down with someone over me had always been a real problem.

Dr. Winters's conclusion was that I had some real spiritual issues. Some of the stuff I must have explained to her was out of her scope of knowledge or formal education, and she did not feel comfortable advising me about these issues. Dr. Winters was not a professed believer in Christ. Although she was very intrigued with what I knew and the story I had, she could not guide me toward the kind of help I needed. She simply didn't have the spiritual resources.

I continued to escape either through work, daily activities, busyness, or some form of entertainment. Maggie said often that she had never seen anyone with such a spiritual struggle and battle. She fervently continued to seek help from many sources both within the United States and outside the country for someone who could offer insight into how to get relief for me. The adversary had such a grip on me that it appeared I would never escape his grasp.

I enjoyed the conflict with Christians and the available power I had earned on the dark side. That power was the real addiction that was so very hard to release. That was the link that held me in bondage.

✝

While I was at home and off the road, I was in the home improvement centers daily with the many projects I had going on. In one of the stores, a Home Depot, I always saw a man who worked there. In fact, I sought him out. I never really talked to him, but I would follow him around the store as he worked. I wasn't quite sure why I did it, other than I wanted something he had. A huge spiritual presence surrounded him, opposite of what surrounded me. His name was Chris Beall. As he worked, I got as physically close to him as I could. I went from aisle to aisle as he helped customers and worked on inventory. I was intrigued with the positive spiritual aura that surrounded him. Chris never really knew my motives and why I was always coming so near to where he was in the store; however, he did often ask if I needed help finding something.

At the time I didn't realize this was a very trying time in

Chris's life. He was battling personal problems. From what I witnessed and from my spiritual perspective, he possessed such integrity and honor. The spiritual light that was around him was one of the most magnificent and concentrated I had seen. I wondered why a hedge of protection was around this man; I was very intrigued. I continued following him around that store for nearly a year, not to interfere with his job but to learn from him (from observation). I was in a constant state of learning, no matter the subject. I soaked up most sensory input; I analyzed everything around me. I was highly sensitive to both the spiritual and physical world, and at times, it wore me out.

CHAPTER 8

THE BATTLE INTENSIFIES

The night is nearly over; the day is almost here. So let us put aside the deeds of darkness and put on the armor of light.

—ROMANS 13:12

As soon as David Barnes and I drove away from our offices to start our business trip, I started to question why I had brought him. He was a new employee, and at times we got along, and at times it was as if we would kill each other. He stared out of my truck passenger side window and off into contemplative thought a great deal. That intrigued me because I liked deep thinkers, but what was he thinking about?

As we drove, I became increasingly torn between liking and hating him, and I started to become more agitated and angry. I tried not to show my emotions and was fairly good at hiding the darkness within me. My spiritual father was the father of lies, and I relied heavily on his guidance and protection. David's spiritual father was the Father of light, and he was relying on his God to guide and protect him. How strange, two grown men in the cab of a pickup, having two different masters they turned to for guidance and direction. The farther we drove, the smaller the cab seemed to get!

We had a similar agenda. Turn to our god, influence the

other person, and see where the day took us. Both of us were very patient men, both deep thinkers, both determined.

The internal and spiritual battles continued in the cab for three days while we were on the road. Not much happened outwardly until an incident occurred at a gas station where we stopped for fuel.

A few days before this trip, my daughter Kristin had given me a coin and asked me to keep it with me at all times. It was metal and about three times the size of a quarter. On one side was a Christian cross, and on the other was an inscribed prayer asking God to bless her earthly father and be with him always. I carried it everywhere for sentimental reasons. Even though I did not know the God she did, I kept it on me because it reminded me of her. The coin she gave me was always in my left pocket with my other loose change. I pulled it out frequently to look at it.

We parked at the pumps of the gas station, and I began to fuel the truck. David and I decided to go into the store to get a Coke. We made our selections and proceeded to the register to pay. The store had several cashiers and was full of customers, probably twelve or so, at the time. I went up to the front where a younger man, perhaps in his early twenties, manned the cash register. While walking toward the register, I began to fade into the spirit. Meaning, I started to get highly sensitive in the spirit and less aware of my physical existence. Matters and thoughts of the spirit began to take over my thought processes, and my sixth sense went into overdrive. As we engaged, my defenses and spiritual awareness heightened. He greeted me in a normal fashion but seemed a little disturbed.

I pulled out change from my jeans pocket to buy a Coke and box of chocolate donuts. As I looked at this man, I noticed his scarred arms. He looked down at my left arm and noticed the scars and the blessing coin in my hand—writing side up, cross side down. Everything at this moment slowed as I was instantly thrust into the spirit. Everyone in the store, including David, seemed to be moving in slow motion. Their speech was very pronounced, drawn out of them slowly, and distorted but decipherable. I looked around the store in a defense mode and was convinced that no one there could harm me.

I turned back to the young man helping me at the register. His voice changed. It was deeper and scratchy. He looked at me, his eyes turning red, and said, "What is that coin?"

I said, "Oh, it's a God thing."

He then abruptly and loudly said, "Satan wants you back. You are going to die."

As I again turned to look at the other patrons, it seemed everyone in the store had heard these comments. Some were frightened; others had inquisitive looks on their faces. I looked at David.

David was wide-eyed and inquired, "What did he say?"

As I looked back at the man, he and I were the only ones going at what seemed a normal speed; everyone else in the store seemed to be speaking and living in slow motion. I took the coin and flipped it to its other side, which displayed the cross. I confidently smirked as I said, "Not this time. I will cross over!" Although I really wasn't thinking I'd do any such thing, especially since I thought Christianity was for the weak of mind, the kid had angered me some. Bottom line: I wasn't afraid to die.

As he tried to stare me down and transfer spirits, I left the store with David following behind. David was amazed, though shaken. He asked me to clarify my conversation with the man. I shared with him what we had said, although he had heard the conversation well and just wanted assurance that what he heard was what was really said!

As we approached the truck to leave, the man was yelling at me in the overhead speaker that was placed under the gas pump canopy.

The man yelled, "You heard me!"

I was certain it was the voice of Satan proceeding out of his mouth. The words were like venom, scratchy and viperous. As we drove away, David had a puzzled look on his face and fidgeted for his phone. This incident was over. I drove away.

We were in New Mexico at the time, and as David was praying under his breath, I became nervous. I was driving and faded into the spirit. I no longer noticed David was sitting next to me. Without conscious thought, I pulled out a sharp pocketknife with my right hand and was in the process of cutting my left arm as we drove down the highway. I felt the need to usher in some support from the spirit realm. This was a fairly typical event, when I felt the need to recruit spiritual help for whatever reason. It wasn't a cry in the flesh as much as a cry in the spirit. I didn't care who was around and wasn't doing it for effect or attention. In fact, the deeper I got into the satanic in the later years, the more oblivious I was to the external goings-on and more acutely aware of the spiritual aspects of my life.

I am not sure what happened next, but the knife was gone and I was pulled over behind a small gas station. David was outside the cab, on his phone. Everything was a little foggy to me as he entered the cab and we proceeded down the highway. I found out David had me pull over at the gas station so that he could call a well-known lady in his church for prayer support. This lady was accustomed to these experiences in her counseling ministry. He was ready to walk home and run away from the bizarre events he saw take place on this trip. David decided to hang with me with much prayer support from his friends and continue with a wild ride back home.

The trip lasted a day or two longer, and we returned home with little or no spiritual occurrence that I know of.

✝

The next day after the road trip, I was back at the office and at my desk. I kept hearing strange sounds from David's office, demonic in nature, moans and cries for help, and many conversations, as if a dozen people were in his office, all talking at one time. I peered around the corner and looked into his room. He was quietly working at his desk and didn't see me peer his way. The later in the day it got, the angrier and more agitated I became. I don't recall all the reasons why, but I was thinking about David and my road trip and in addition was dwelling on a new thought: I felt that David had been secretly disrespecting me in front of my employees, contractors, and girlfriend.

I had always conversed under my breath with the adversary and didn't realize that soon what was in my heart would come out of my mouth. I approached David's office, where many employees were standing around talking. In a fairly loud tone I said, "You got my back, Satan" (not realizing I had said it out loud and many heard it). I said that kind of thing a lot in my head for several years when I was about to harass Christians, fight, or do the devil's bidding, but this time I blurted it out loud. I peered at David, who was at his desk, yelled profanities at him, threatened him with physical harm, and fired him.

The more I sat in the office this day, the more stressed I became. Although I had only been back a day from my trip with David, I quickly decided to hit the road again. I wanted out. I needed alone time and energy, which I seemed to get when I was on the road. I would leave early in the morning.

I left the office and then went home to get my Harley and take a ride on the interstate. I guess traveling on I-35 northbound at a hundred miles per hour on a large motorcycle is one way to clear your head, but even that didn't work this day! After a twenty-mile round-trip jaunt, I returned home and traded the bike for a bed. I'd had enough for one day.

At 8 a.m. I left my Oklahoma home and drove away for what would be another fairly short trip. I would go east to Memphis, Tennessee, and then back home. The total trip should only take me about three days.

Driving out of town, I decided to stop by Barnes & Noble and get a coffee. While I waited for my order, I headed for the New Age section. I glanced down and noticed four copies of the satanic bible on the shelf. I made my way to the register with my copies and checked out. It was common that I bought these books to distribute wherever I was led. I picked up my coffee and left the store.

It was Wednesday, and I was heading east on I-40 to Little Rock, Arkansas, to spend the night. I arrived in Little Rock at 6 p.m. and pulled into a truck stop to get fuel. Reaching for the fuel hose, I looked north and saw a massive colonial structure that appeared to be a church.

As my tank filled with diesel, my head filled with thoughts: *Look at that big steeple. That is one huge church; I wonder what kind it is. Another group of "What Would Jesus Do?" bracelet-wearing believers? I tell you what Jesus would do: He would puke!*

That steeple is an outward sign of faith to the outside world, yet, I guarantee inside that church is another bunch of lukewarm Christians. What is a Christian anyway? That term doesn't mean a thing. What is the difference between a Satanist and a lukewarm Christian? Nothing.

In a few minutes, I was parking my truck and trailer in the parking lot of the huge church. I jumped from the truck, stuffed all four satanic bibles into my coat pocket, and headed for the front doors of the church. People were entering the church, as services would begin shortly. Several men at the front door welcomed everyone who entered. I avoided their handshakes and their greetings.

My first stop was the back pew to watch those entering and to scope out the type of church I was in. My objective was to get out of the church before praise and worship started. I pulled out a satanic bible and placed it in the pew pocket. I immediately stood and crossed the aisle and walked ten rows forward toward the altar. A lady sat directly in front of the pew I chose. I placed a bible under the pew where she sat and with my foot slid the bible between her feet.

I rose and went outside before the service started. As I exited, a greeter asked if everything was okay. I answered, "Oh, it is perfect."

I walked toward my truck and went past the elementary portion of the church school. I threw a satanic bible under a bench outside one of the classrooms. Closer to my truck, I took another bible and stuck it on a window ledge outside another grade school room. I made my way to the truck and drove off. My actions may seem somewhat juvenile, especially for a forty-nine-year old man, but it was just the contrary: it was my assignment. Satan had given me a mission to disrupt churches and lead believers astray, to draw the weak away from the flock, if you will.

The god I served assured me that intrigue in the dark side has always been the real lure for mankind. I sensed the dark spirits urging me to "get them while they are young" (meaning physically and spiritually). In Satan's eyes, the loss of innocence is the beginning of the war. When there are no more innocent children, he will reign.

So what might seem like a childish prank or not-so-innocent fun was actually a diabolical plan to disrupt, instill fear, and wreak havoc on churches, with spiritual murder as the goal.

✝

I drove onto I-40 and headed east. About five miles out of town, I noticed a guy with a green backpack walking slowly down the shoulder of the highway. As I passed by, I slowed down when he stared at me in an inquisitive way. It wasn't my habit to pick up hitchhikers; nevertheless I pulled my rig onto the shoulder about an eighth of a mile from the man and waited for him to walk up to the truck.

As he climbed into the truck I said, "Hey, dude, where are you headed?"

The man, who appeared to be in his midthirties, politely said, "Nowhere, really."

"I'm Mike. What's your name?"

"Mark."

I immediately felt a rush of peace come over me. Mark sat and buckled himself in and set his backpack between his feet on the floorboard. He then asked me, "Where are you headed?"

"Nowhere, really," I responded.

As I accelerated back onto the highway, I asked, "What's in the backpack?"

Mark looked as though he had to reflect on the answer, as if he were carrying on two conversations and my question jolted him from thought.

He answered, "Bibles. They are Bibles."

Not the answer I expected. I had expected tattered clothes in there and a few belongings, maybe with a sad story about homelessness, loneliness, and an eventual request for money.

Mark looked a bit weathered, but he was clean and extremely calm. He also looked as though he was accustomed to traveling. His demeanor indicated his being one in charge and confident.

Mark then asked me, "What do you have in your briefcase?"

I answered, "Bibles. Just bibles."

Although I had only bought four satanic bibles at Barnes & Noble and had passed those out at the church earlier, I always had a few stashed in my briefcase in my truck.

Our eyes met as Mark asked again, "Where are you headed?"

"Man, I can take that question a few different ways. Who's asking?" I responded. Mark's silence led to my adding, "I am going to the East Coast for work purposes."

After another moment or so of silence, I said, "Mark, what do you normally do for income?"

"I travel and love meeting people around the United States. I minister to anyone I meet," he said.

I quickly joked, "Oh, I bet that pays really well!"

But Mark didn't laugh. I glanced at him and saw him looking at me with gentle yet penetrating eyes.

"Michael . . . where are you headed? Can I pray for you?" he asked softly.

I knew in my spirit the first time he asked, "Where are you headed?" that he was thinking in more of a long-term, spiritual sense.

Although I felt a bit uncomfortable with him praying to God in my car, I said, "Okay."

He prayed for my salvation and prayed for my children. He prayed for protection over me and called in angels to guide me. He also prayed that the Lord would forgive me and have mercy on me. When Mark finished praying, he said something to me that I will never forget.

Mark said, "Before you petition my Father who is in heaven, ask Him for forgiveness of your sins and then come to Him with your requests. Michael, you need to read Psalm 91 and memorize it; hide it in your heart. And remember, the wisdom of this world is foolishness to God. You know God because He knew you first."

"Okay . . ." I said, perplexed at the words from this strange hitchhiker. "But how did you know I have children?" I asked.

The cab got silent as we drove another few minutes or so. Finally Mark answered, "I know because God knows." He reached down and grabbed his backpack. "I'd like to get out here if I may, please."

"Are you sure? There is nothing around here but fields, Mark."

"Yes, please."

I pulled the truck over to let him out along the shoulder of the highway. It was dark outside and no houses, buildings, or businesses were around for miles. He assured me, "This will be fine. God bless you, Michael."

"My name is Mike," I reminded him.

He smiled. "God likes your given name, Michael." He closed the door.

I nodded good-bye to Mark and proceeded down the highway. The instant he left, I felt a change of awareness in the cab of the truck. It was not as peaceful or calm. I looked back to get another glance at Mark and did not see him anywhere.

I drove eastward to Memphis and spent the night there. Along the way I thought a lot about Mark and wondered where he went when I let him out of the cab of my truck.

I awoke the next morning and completed the jobs I had lined up for the day. About 1 p.m., after having finished my last job, I turned the truck west and headed home. I had the next twelve hours or so to contemplate one particular pastor who had been on my mind a lot lately.

CHAPTER 9

A MISSION OF MURDER

For the word of God is alive and active. Sharper than any double-edged sword, it penetrates even to dividing soul and spirit, joints and marrow; it judges the thoughts and attitudes of the heart. Nothing in all creation is hidden from God's sight. Everything is uncovered and laid bare before the eyes of him to whom we must give account.

—HEBREWS 4:12–13

During some of my darkest hours and during the time I lived on Oak Creek Drive, Maggie started taking my daughter Kristin to LifeChurch.tv, a nondenominational church whose senior pastor is Craig Groeschel. LifeChurch was one of the fastest-growing churches in the country, and its ministry was gaining in popularity and influence in Oklahoma City and beyond. Kristin and Maggie spoke highly of their experiences at LifeChurch and how much they respected Pastor Craig and his ministry. They loved his messages, his unabashed commitment to Christ, and his willingness to challenge the culture and to confront issues that many church leaders shied away from.

The more they gushed about Craig and LifeChurch, the more agitated I became. As their appreciation for Craig's ministry and leadership became more enthusiastic, my anger toward Craig grew into resentment. Finally, this disdain for him and his church became a source of unholy obsession, a fixation that was troubling even by my standards. My descent into the dark arts was accelerating at a rapid pace, and Satan's grip on my life was tightening, so much so that I was about to graduate spiritually. A special assignment was about to be given to me.

✝

Although my work often kept me away for weeks at a time, one particular evening I was in town, working on my own house, when strange, unearthly sounds emanated from the walls of the master bedroom. Scratching on the Sheetrock and guttural groans grabbed my full attention. I tried to dismiss it as night sounds and continued working until the low hum of baritone chanting began to fill the room. With wet hands and a pounding heart, I had an impulse to run due to the intensity of the visitation (the strongest I'd had up to this point). The demonic sounds from the unholy choir directed me to the living room. On wobbly legs, I shuffled to the living room, where I was engulfed by an evil presence. As this darkness surrounded me, my will became overpowered. Then I made another tragic mistake as I knelt in obedience to this hellish force.

On my knees, I felt a heavy presence surround me and then an indwelling. It was made clear to me that this was a death spirit. This spirit gave me a mission, and as certain as the words you are reading right now, his message was clear: *"Kill Craig Groeschel."* The satanic spirit further explained that another man had been given this task and had run from the responsibility. Others made idle threats but were only seeking attention and notoriety. I was now the chosen one.

The task would not be simple. Patience and calculated effort were needed to infiltrate the church's security and accomplish my assigned mission, but what a coup for the army of darkness as a great man of God and his ministry would be ruined. Not to mention my personal windfall: increased spiritual power. The desire for more spiritual strength stirred my flesh and only made me lust for more. The fear I felt earlier due to the overwhelming presence of such an evil force subsided. The thirst for power masked any fear left in me.

†

Maggie was thrilled at my sudden interest in attending church services with her and Kristin. Her desire to see me experience spiritual recovery was so strong that I knew she'd be willing to overlook the embarrassing stunts I'd pulled in every church we attended over the last few years. I had been rude, disruptive, and a general nuisance in other churches to the point that we were invariably asked to leave and not come back. But I knew she'd overlook every callow stunt I'd pulled in hopes that her hopeless boyfriend could know true hope. Her concern fed right into Satan's plan since LifeChurch.tv was exactly where Satan wanted me, to fulfill my murderous mission.

When I first darkened the door of LifeChurch, in the fall of 2005, the building was still in a development stage. Its main auditorium, where services are held today, was under construction, giving the impression of a growing church body.

Entering the bustling church foyer, I found crowds of people gathered between services, sipping coffee, smiling, and laughing. I was nauseated as I watched friends greet each other warmly with sincere, "How are ya, brother?" backslapping, and warm handshakes. *Why are they here? What is compelling them to act this way toward each other?* Like a foreigner in a strange country, I stood dumbfounded at this open expression of love and joy. Perhaps it was the largest gathering I had been to, or somehow I was "seeing" more at this time. I wasn't certain as I gazed at the massive crowd.

I hid my repulsion by keeping a comfortable distance, making no eye contact, and limiting my interaction with everyone. The only tipping of my hand of my new assignment and reason in visiting the church were e-mails I sent to my daughter and others, expressing my dislike for Craig. However, at the time, I was flying under the radar, a secret agent with an unholy mission to assassinate an enemy of darkness. I intended to complete this mission.

I would not venture into the sanctuary, even after the new auditorium was complete. I not only felt out of place spiritually but was physically and spiritually uncomfortable when I was anywhere near the doors of the sanctuary.

I followed the same drill every week: I armed myself with a 9mm and two clips, which I hid under my shirt and tucked away in the rear waistband of my pants. I sat out in the foyer, drank coffee, ate doughnuts, and watched security. I studied their movements, became familiar with their routines, and tried to find their weaknesses. The vulnerability of most churches is quite alarming. Some have volunteer staff and possibly paid security, most of whom are lulled into a tranquil routine from Sunday to Sunday. But LifeChurch was different, making my job more difficult. Security at LifeChurch was heightened due to earlier threats, and it boasted well-organized and coordinated security personnel led by a capable man named John Zeigler.

Killing a high-profile figure would be a daunting task, but the spiritual influences in my life urged me on. *"You can do this." "You are stronger than the rest." "You will be rewarded."* These and other demonic voices echoed through my head as the scheme took shape. I didn't care if I took the pastor out in public or private; the outcome was all that was important.

The plainclothes security were in the same place, same seats, Sunday after Sunday. I sensed their boredom and their thoughts: *I wish I was home with my family. I hate working on Sundays.* As the weeks progressed, they seemed to be getting weaker and more lackadaisical. I was getting stronger and more determined.

After a full year of patient observation, the day for me to fulfill my mission was fast approaching. While the inside of LifeChurch was an atmosphere of holiness, fellowship, praise, and worship, on the outside of the church, dark and ominous forces were stirring. Satan's forces gathered in a fury of anticipation and gleeful excitement over what would soon happen: the shattered lives, a crippled ministry, and the thousands whose spiritual futures would be negatively impacted. The underworld was alive and crackling with black-hearted laughter at the prospects of so much pain and suffering. I saw fallen angels with perverse smiles, rubbing their hands incessantly, lusting for the ensuing pain. Their dark presence guided, goaded, and urged me on like a bloodthirsty mob in a Roman coliseum, screaming for the blood of a Christian.

As the day grew near, I became more agitated and restless. But my lord was the father of lies, and he'd trained me well. I steeled myself and was determined to hide any anxiety or nervousness that would give me away. I masked all that was stirring inside of me: the growing rage, the desire for more stature in the underworld, a desire to unleash a wave of suffering into the lives of everyone who called this church home. No one in my life knew of this wicked scheme, though Maggie, my daughter, and a few others did sense the Holy Spirit alerting them to a spiritual battle that was being played out in my life. I believe they sensed the stakes and began to intervene.

Each Sunday morning, Kristin would ask me, "Why don't you come sit with us during the service, Dad? You don't need to sit out here." And each Sunday, I would reject her invitation and sit outside the worship service instead.

Maggie was equally concerned. She said, "Mike, I know there are some men in this church who would really like to get to know you. Why don't we join a life group? I think it would help." But I would have none of it.

†

Finally, the day had come. I sensed a surge of demonic power that Sunday morning and knew that this was the day to carry out the mission of murder that Satan had given to me. Today was the day to snuff the life of Craig Groeschel. It was also the day I was prepared to die.

It was about 8 a.m. when I got out of bed. As on every other Sunday morning, Maggie had already gotten up and was preparing for the day and putting her makeup on.

"Did you rest well?" she said.

As I jumped into the shower, I said, "It was rest enough. It's going to be a great day today!"

"Good," she replied.

I took an unusually long shower and soaked under the pressure of the hot water as it massaged my skin. I thought about how I was going to slip past security and take Craig out. It was simple: I would wait until after services and hide on the east side of the building, close to the doors he exited to get to his truck and leave. When he came out, I would wait until he was a few feet away from the door and fire. His security was usually facing him and not looking behind.

I had watched the security guards many times from my parked car. Those guys looked forward and left to right, but never behind where they had just been. Why? There was no need. They were just there, and they must have thought there was no way someone could ever slip behind them. However, just thirty feet or so away was the northeast corner of the building, where there was no sentry. The huge generator there would help mask any unusual sound coming from the corner of the building, like my footsteps.

My thoughts continued as I left the shower and entered the closet to dry off and get dressed. I thought of each step I needed to take to be totally prepared. In the time it took to get dressed, I had played the whole scene in my mind at least ten times. As I did so, I took my gun from my underwear drawer and placed it under a pair of pants I had on a shelf. I also took an extra clip and placed it with the gun. I had loaded the "magic bullet" I intended to use on Craig in the top spot in the first clip that was already in place in the gun.

After I was dressed, I went outside to feed the koi in the pond and take a last look at the backyard I had put so much work into during the past four years or so. I came back in the house to hear Maggie saying that we were running late and we needed to hurry. With a final look at the home I would probably never see again,

I scurried quickly behind her, and we were out of the house and down the street, headed for church.

Not much was said as Maggie talked on the phone with one of her children, and I was near numb with thought and anticipation of the events that would occur within a few hours.

✝

We arrived at church, and I knew there was only an hour or so for Craig, and probably me, to live. I took my regular spot in the foyer as Maggie went into church.

While I waited for an opportunity to outmaneuver security and put a bullet in the pastor's head, something happened. As I watched Craig's message through the closed-circuit televisions, heard the reading of God's holy Word and the songs of praise come floating through, it hit me like a bolt of lightning through the forehead. What was protecting this church wasn't a security detail with their firepower and video cameras. It was the Word of God being spoken aloud and the praises from His people. These were the real weapons that were protecting the church and its pastor. Those words did not go void into nothingness, nor did they in my spirit. For some reason, I started to hear the message. I started to see the televisions. The message of the gospel began to pierce my wicked heart, and Satan and his demonic lackeys were helpless against it. They had no defense against God's power that was being projected into my life. The bulwark that Satan had successfully erected around my heart and that had blocked the prayers of many faithful saints was being dismantled, and the light of heaven began its transformative work in me.

As I sat shell-shocked in the foyer of this church, an usher whose name I don't remember came by to say hello. In my trance-like state, I proceeded to tell him the history of my dark and lonely past. It flowed out of me like a wild river undammed. My plan to put a gun to Craig's head and take his life that morning, as well as graphic details of my satanic rituals, were only a few of the horrid tales that spewed from my mouth.

After several minutes, I looked up and saw the usher, who stood speechless, his eyes like saucers, staring at me in surprise and horror. Not realizing the magnitude of what I'd just done, I noticed Maggie coming out of the sanctuary. I quickly said good-bye to the usher and joined Maggie in her car. We drove away. I told her nothing about that conversation, mostly because I didn't recall what I had said.

While I was inside the church, revealing Satan's plan to a stranger, outside the forces of darkness that guided me were irate. Not only had I failed in my mission, but I had crossed a boundary. I'd fraternized with the enemy. I'd made a blood covenant with the prince of darkness, and now it was *my* blood he wanted for willful disobedience. I had put myself in a dangerous position and was teetering on the edge of death. Physical death to a betrayer was attached to the blood pact I had made; it was just an inherent part of this type of spiritual contract. I now awakened somehow to the gravity of the decision I had made nearly twenty years earlier. But, it didn't matter much. Not in the state I was now in, as despair and hopelessness continued to take over my very soul.

I can't imagine how the usher's explanation of my bizarre ramblings sounded in the retelling, but he must have done an adequate job, because as I learned later, that week my picture was posted in the staff rooms of every LifeChurch campus in the city.

The caption read, "If you see this man, call security . . . call the police." Within the church, I was now a wanted criminal.

I tried to carry on normally the following week, but life became more troubling. If something could go wrong, it did. The business I owned was failing. Maggie and I were living lives anchored mostly by business and financial ties. My depression overwhelmed me. The days passed slowly as each moment was consumed with a cascade of negative thoughts.

Unaware of the wanted posters on the church walls, I agreed to attend LifeChurch the following week with Maggie. But now, with my defenses shattered, new thoughts and questions pounded my mind; visions of death and an unthinkable afterlife. Flashes of light penetrated my heart. My mind absorbed enough truth to begin to doubt the darkness that enslaved me.

What am I really seeking? Can I be reached? Does God care about me at all? Is God really love? Is it possible, really possible, that God isn't both good and evil? Could it be that I was created for more than just pain and suffering? I recalled how at the end of each service Craig would always say, "None of us is good enough; none of us is worthy; none of us has gone too far." But I'd gone so far!

With these conflicting thoughts swirling in my mind, I walked through the doors of the church. Maggie headed for the sanctuary, while I headed for the coffee and a secluded spot. With coffee in hand, I sat on a window ledge in the western foyer of the church. I looked up and saw a sign that said, "By entering this place your bags are subject to inspection. By being here you are subject to being photographed." I seemed to focus on everything that caught my eye. Things that had always been there, but it was as if I noticed the physical attributes of the building for the first time. My focus previously had always been on the spiritual surroundings of the church and of the attendees. Now I began to hyperfocus on the simple, tangible objects that surrounded me.

I suddenly realized I had forgotten to arm myself before leaving the house.

I looked out the window into the sky. Clouds passed overhead as I stared into the distance, trying to ease the rush of anxiety and sense of helplessness. As my mind began to drift with the clouds, an armed deputy sheriff tapped me on the shoulder.

"Are you Mike Leehan?"

"Yes," I replied.

"You need to come with me." He ushered me into the main offices, where I was joined by several officers and a couple of staff members, including the campus pastor, Chris Spradlin.

Attention was focused on me as head of security John Zeigler asked, "Mike, do you have any weapons on you?"

Surprisingly, I remained calm during this confrontation. I looked at John and thought, *He's a big guy, but I'm not afraid of him physically.* After my years in spiritual bondage, physical pain meant nothing to me. I relied more on my spiritual prowess than I did my physical attributes in such an environment.

As I surveyed the room, I sensed weaknesses and I saw confusion and heaviness on several faces. I saw a lack of understanding regarding spiritual gifts. With my gift of spiritual knowledge, I saw experiences and events that were going to take place in the next year or so. I saw vulnerabilities and opportunities for future disruption. However, I also perceived a pure faith that was disarming. I saw a glimpse into the lives of several men in the room and was drawn to the love they exuded.

"No, I have no weapons," I replied in an even tone to John.

The men sat around me as Chris took a chair opposite me. I was now cornered and under their authority. I felt vulnerable and trapped. In a moment I was transformed from a man who acted instantly based on higher-level awareness fueled by evil, to one who was strangely inhibited by some external force. I later realized the force was love.

"Why are you here at LifeChurch today, Mike?" Chris inquired.

As he questioned me, I couldn't control my thoughts. I began channeling and finally went blank.

Channeling is the practice of speaking with spirit guides and communicating with the dead . . . and zoning out. Mediums and psychics use this technique, as well as some satanists. It involves intense concentration and focus and often leads to an out-of-body experience. I used channeling as a means to gain insight into people I had to confront to gain an upper hand or to escape Christian overload when I was in the vicinity of too many Christians. I always felt heaviness around them.

I became present again and said, "I'm not here for what you think."

Chris locked eyes with several other men and then looked at me. "Then why are you here? From what I understand, it is to harm a certain staff member."

I looked straight at him. I am certain Mr. Spradlin and staff had no realization of the actual threat I had been to the church and staff over the past year until my outpouring to the usher last week.

Although I had been in and out of channeling up to this point, I was back totally in the present. I imagine from the looks on the faces of several men there that they were wondering what the heck was going on with me. Typically during a channeling session, I would look straight ahead with a blank stare and would be almost in a semiconscious state, as others who witnessed it have told me. I imagined this is what these men saw, as when I "came to," their expressions indicated such. I felt very weak physically at this point.

I answered Mr. Spradlin, "I'm done with that. I think I am seeking freedom from the life I've been living for so long. I think I'm seeking your God. I'm just not sure what to do next. I just need some time . . . and a little space."

Chris looked at me with contemplative eyes and said, "I don't know, bud. I need time to think about this and talk to staff members and see what we should do. And mostly, we need to seek God's will in this." He reached for a sheet of paper. "Give me a number where you can be reached, and I will call you after we meet this week to discuss you. You need to leave the church grounds now."

I nodded and gave him my cell phone number. "You won't have to worry about this much longer. If I am pursuing your God, I won't be alive for long."

The men ushered me outside and to my car. While I waited for Maggie, I analyzed all my weaknesses in the meeting. I felt helpless and lost, especially when I considered the stark spiritual differences between me and the men in that room. They clearly had something I didn't have, and for the first time in my life, I was sincerely curious about it. I wondered if Chris would ever call me. I wondered what was next.

I wondered if I would be alive tomorrow. The spiritual world and the god I was serving didn't take lightly to followers leaving.

Once a blood covenant was made, the chance of surviving leaving that covenant was very slim. Most lost souls who served the underworld and Satan, like Judas who betrayed Jesus, self-exterminate. Few get out alive.

Finally, the service was over and the crowds poured out of the church building. Unaware of my meeting with security, Maggie approached the car and said, "Did you enjoy the service?"

I could tell by her upbeat demeanor that she had no clue of what I just went through. I answered, "Oh yeah, the coffee was great."

"Good. Ready to go?"

"Yup."

We drove home with little said. Maggie talked on her cell phone with a friend, and my mind was consumed with what just transpired. I was amazed that I was allowed to leave the property. I was surprised that the staff at the church didn't have me detained and arrested. *If they had really known the threat I had been, and for so long, they would have called outside authorities,* I thought. *Are they following us now? Is Maggie part of all this, and I am not aware? Is Kristin involved in my getting busted, even though she wasn't at service today? I bet I never return there again.*

My thoughts continued until we arrived home.

†

Monday rolled around, and as I was outside my house, cleaning in the garden, a couple of Jehovah's Witnesses approached me.

"What's going on, guys?" I said in a polite tone. They smiled, and we chatted a little while about God and the Scripture. Finally one of them cocked his head and said, "You sure do know a lot of Scripture. You must be a believer."

I shook my head. "No, I've been worshipping Satan a long time. I learned some Scripture along the way."

I thought my mentioning satanism would scare them away; instead, it just intrigued them in a way that kept them coming back whenever they were in the neighborhood. In my mind, they were just like every other person in my life trying to win me over to their God; I was just a notch in their belt if they could succeed, a story they could share with their friends.

After the two Witnesses left, I continued the yard work with an increasing sense of emptiness. The ringing cell phone pulled me from my thoughts.

"This is Mike," I answered.

"Mike, this is Chris Spradlin, from LifeChurch."

"Yeah, hey, Chris." I tried to sound unruffled. I couldn't believe he'd called so quickly but assumed he was going to tell me that I would never be allowed to set foot inside of LifeChurch again.

"Listen, Mike, I had a chance to talk to our senior staff, and I want you to know that you are welcome at LifeChurch at any time. On one condition: you need to text John Zeigler on Sunday morning and let him know which service you're going to be attending. John will be watching you."

I was dumbstruck. "Okay," I managed to say.

"And, Mike," Chris continued in a kind tone, "if you enter the sanctuary, you will need to sit in the same place every Sunday and conduct yourself in a way that would be pleasing to God. That's all we're asking."

"Okay, Chris . . . thanks."

"And if you need anything from me, don't hesitate to ask. God bless you, Mike."

My head was swimming. Did Chris just say that I could come back to the church? There was no pressure, no forced meetings, no radical deliverance offered, just the simple and reasonable instructions to sit down and act right.

I couldn't believe it. The church welcomed me back, but whenever I entered, I knew there would be many sets of eyes on me . . . and rightfully so.

☩

In the fall of 2006, Maggie and I started attending a life group on Wednesday nights at the home of Kristie Warren. Life groups are home Bible study groups that meet weekly for study and fellowship. The first night I went, three women were present: Kristie Warren (the host) and two others; they were all single and attractive. The Bible teacher was Jim VanDerwiele, the only married person in the group. I sensed a spiritual presence as I first walked into Kristie's house and am quite certain that they did as well. I was later told that the three women started praying immediately when I explained portions of my life in introductions and discussions. Everything seemed to pour out of me . . . again.

In Kristie, I sensed a genuine heart for people. She was independent, gentle, and kind. I loved that she was so accepting and accommodating. Through the course of the evening, I came to find out she was a businesswoman and owned her own copier and computer service company. She was also an accomplished carpenter. She had more carpentry tools than I did, which I found fascinating. I liked her right away.

Our teacher, Jim, was very insightful, and I could tell by

talking with him that he was steady in his faith and had been teaching for quite some time. His straightforward teaching and the gentle manner in which he handled questions from the group was calming for me. Although Jim attended a fairly conservative church, he believed in the gifts of the Spirit and was open to hearing about my past and present spiritual experiences, although perhaps somewhat cautiously. LifeChurch encouraged their life groups to be all about community, so people from different churches or denominations were welcomed.

In reflecting on my own life experiences, education, and spiritual walk, the more I learned, the more I realized I didn't know. It's a humbling truth—and humility of spirit is something I recognized in Jim immediately. I believed his wisdom and experience would give him insight into my life. One of the young women was at the point I deemed to be the typical or average Christian. She seemed dedicated to her faith, but I could see heaviness about her as she struggled with worldly desires as most young or noncommitted Christians do. She appeared to be a fence-sitter, so to speak. With a heavy foot in the world, she also went to church regularly.

You see, my gift of discernment could make me very destructive in these environments, as I had the ability to "read" people and understand their struggles, but I didn't have the Holy Spirit directing me . . . quite the opposite. In the past, this woman would have been a prime target for manipulation, but at this juncture, I was cautiously seeking freedom from darkness and paid little attention to her. She seemed like a whole lot of trouble to me.

The next woman present was very attractive, but it wasn't her looks that drew me in. It was her joyful spirit that intrigued me. I noticed her praying under her breath as she looked at me. I stared back, sizing her up. I focused on her blue eyes and saw strength in her and also some pain that I couldn't pin down. I tried to get into this woman's head but was strangely shut out.

✝

I continued my weekly visits with Maggie to Kristie's home group and was regularly doing my "lobby only" services at LifeChurch. About four weeks into my new relationship with the church, I was doing my typical coffee-drinking alone, watching the eyes that were watching me, and keeping a safe distance.

This Sunday, Maggie went into service and came out seconds later to mention that the sanctuary was cold inside and to ask if I would bring her another cup of coffee in ten to fifteen minutes. I agreed. I had never entered into the sanctuary before, and after about ten minutes of anxious anticipation, I opened the doors and eased my way in. Maggie told me where she would be sitting, and I spotted her in the crowd.

I walked down the aisle with frayed nerves. I did not want to walk halfway through the church to reach her, but I did. I handed her the coffee.

"You want to stay?" she asked with a glint of hope.

"No." I headed for the back doors. I exhaled in relief when I exited to the foyer.

It felt so heavy in the sanctuary. Although I was finished with most of the rituals I had become accustomed to in my life, at this period, I was exhausted in every way. This was a very heavy double-minded period. I hadn't given up the satanic totally because that was where I had derived power in the past. However, the more I was around Christians and their habitat, the more the god I served (and his minions) was creating havoc in my life. I was making an effort to change, and the combination of being in both realms created a fierce battle inside of my soul and spirit.

For the next month, every Sunday was the same. I would go into church, be watched, and drink coffee in the back. Maggie continued to ask me to bring her coffee, and I slowly found comfort in my ability to come and go at will. This freedom is what I needed. It would prove to be the key that would eventually unlock the chains that held me in bondage.

Even with my gift of discernment, I was almost always blinded to particular aspects of my own life. I didn't see so much of the mess I was in and the inevitable dilemmas and trials that lay ahead of me. However, during this period, I began to tie together Maggie's asking me to come into the sanctuary and her quest to seek my freedom from the satanic presence in my life. Like a shell-shocked serviceman in the heat of battle, I missed how close to danger I was. I started to see the depth of Maggie's commitment to find help. Her mission to help me find hope was becoming apparent.

One Sunday, I took Maggie her cup of coffee and sat down in the service for a minute. Still uncomfortable and with my stomach in knots, I listened as Craig taught on the supernatural.

Craig asked, "Is anyone hearing from Satan right now? Is Satan speaking to you?"

I was not certain if Craig asked this because he had seen me or if it was just in the big spiritual scheme that was playing out in my life. My thoughts continued. *Certainly he didn't notice me in this huge crowd. And what is the chance of the series he is teaching being called "The Supernatural"? Really? Is that just a coincidence? Is Maggie in on all this? Is she or Kristin part of these bizarre circumstances? Something is up.*

I raised my hand and kept it up. I didn't see another hand raised in the auditorium.

"Thank you, sir," the pastor said.

Craig may have not realized I really was hearing from the adversary right then. The enemy had urged me to leave the minute I sat down. After this brief exchange with Craig, I did just that. In fact, I left the building and was near my car, listening to the service through the outdoor speakers in the parking lot, when Craig delivered his altar call.

I sensed that God was speaking directly to me. Although I felt a tug on my heart, I didn't respond. I felt a demonic stirring around me, a dark energy and a sense of urgency. I knew I had tested the spirits and was scared about what might be next. My current, miserable condition propelled me toward a hopeless future. I'd made some small overtures toward a God I wasn't sure existed, and as a result, my small part of the underworld was in an uproar.

Trapped in a spiritual vise that tightened by the day, I didn't know how much more I could take. Something had to give.

☩

Weeks passed and I continued my church visits but found myself unsettled, torn, and more discontented than ever. A battle was raging. I shut out the world and began that everdangerous turning toward isolation and darkness. The stage was being set for my demise, and although things had been going gray for quite some time, I began to notice it more at this time. Craig and the church began to fade. My kids started to fade. Everyone and everything in my life grew colorless as the conflict within me grew more intense. *What is going on? Why have I lost control? What do I really believe in?* Questions bombarded my mind.

Sunday church attendance had become a habit for me in the last three months or so, and I was actually drawn to some of the people there. I envied the peace I saw flowing out of them. Their joyful spirits that at one time would have antagonized me were now attracting me. The enthusiasm they had for life, as though some unseen force was lightening their loads, was still a mystery to me; but it intrigued me. What a contrast to the burden I carried as I trudged through life, fearful, broken, and defeated. The light they emitted began to make me consider that a different way might be possible . . . even for me.

One Sunday, as I walked through the foyer, deep in thought, my head hung low, I glanced up and saw Chris Spradlin standing in front me. He smiled wide and said, "Hey, dude, how are you? Glad to see you."

"Glad to be here, Chris." My response was sincere, but despair was etched all over my face.

Chris knew I was suffering. He looked concerned. "Is there anything I can do for you?"

I shook my head in despair. "I think I am going to die soon. I don't think you understand what's going on or where I've been. This battle is consuming me. I don't see any way out."

Chris stepped forward and put his hand on my shoulder. "There is a way, Mike. There is peace. Jesus is the answer." I looked at Chris and saw the sincerity in his face, the compassion in his eyes. I longed for the peace he had.

"I don't know how I'm going to make it, but I can't take that step yet."

I was unaware a concerned Maggie was behind me and had overheard part of our conversation. Maggie blurted, "Mike, how low do you want to sink? You're at the end. You've been in turmoil your whole life. How much more can one man take? Submit to Jesus, and He will free you from this. Wake up! Listen to Chris! You've been deceived by Satan for so long that you don't know the truth when it's staring you in the face. Satan is killing you. Choose Christ and live."

I came to and realized I had been channeling and had heard just a snippet of what Maggie and Chris were saying. I turned to Chris and said, "I need help."

"Dude, I've never seen anything like this before," he admitted, "but I'll pray with the staff this week on who can best help you. Jesus will get you out of this, Mike."

Chris's attention was soon diverted by several others who were waiting to speak with him, so I said, "Chris, thank you. I appreciate your words."

Maggie and I turned away and walked out of church. We drove home with little said. I was exhausted, and Maggie was exasperated. I spent the rest of the day napping or watching old Westerns on the bedroom TV. Maggie and her children left together and didn't return until late that evening. When they did get back, Maggie went to her office and worked some while the kids went to their bedrooms to do homework and retire. By the time Maggie came back into the house and to our bedroom, I was sound asleep.

✝

Monday morning rolled around, and after the kids went to school and Maggie went to her office, I worked on a couple of business-related items and then took a long ride on the country roads around our house. I was gone for hours only to return to mow, weed-eat, and take care of some outside chores.

That day went by like every other, in a flood of loneliness and despair. But these had been my constant companions for as long as I could remember. I've always felt alone. Now I'd opened the door to spiritual persecution and torment from the master of pain and suffering himself. How could I break through? How could I get rid of this massive oppression? Would I ever have peace? Would I even live?

That evening I found myself in my backyard, watching koi swim in the large pond I'd built a few years earlier. They swam in constant figure eights, circling in and out, round and round, in an endless cycle that would end only upon their death. Whether they were swept up by a hawk that hovered overhead or by a raccoon that ventured by or just grew old and died, their end was inevitable. *Why are they here? Why were they created? Why am I so intrigued with their lives?*

My ringing cell phone pulled me from my contemplation. It was Chris Spradlin.

Chris said he knew a group of men who could help me: a life group called the Damascus Men. He gave me the phone number of the group leader, Darius McGlory, and told me that he had talked with Darius, who was expecting my call. Chris insisted that I call Darius and let him know when I did.

A few weeks passed and life continued its downward spiral. On impulse, I picked up the phone one afternoon and dialed Darius's number. When he answered, I told him who I was, and he told me that Chris had called him and explained what was going on. He assured me that God was working and invited me to come to the men's group that met on Monday nights at a restaurant in downtown Oklahoma City. I agreed.

On each Monday for the past three weeks, I'd circled the block and hadn't managed to get out of the car. But that Monday evening, I finally summoned the courage to stop.

As I walked from my car to the restaurant, I was plagued with negative thoughts about what I was getting ready to experience at the Damascus Men's group. I entered the restaurant, and after I told the host who my party was, he led me to a large meeting room in the rear of the dining area. About thirty men were gathered there. I felt like every set of eyes was on me as I entered. Weathered and worn, beaten and tired, I was a dead man walking. Darius approached me.

"Mike?" I nodded. "What's happening in your life? What's going on with you? He extended his hand, but I wouldn't take it. I hated touch. I hated men who were emotionally open and affectionate. This was not my scene. I refused his hand and paced like a caged animal before finally taking a seat. My stomach knotted as waves of anxiety washed over me. The heavy, suffocating burden I'd felt so many times in the LifeChurch sanctuary began to weigh on me again.

I finally found the strength to sit down and began to share my story with Darius and another man, Frank Stotts, who was persistent in joining the conversation. Both listened carefully to my sordid history, and then Darius said, "Mike, you're welcome here no matter what you've done in your past. The choice is yours, but I hope you come back." I nodded, softening a little.

Then Frank asked, "Mike, can we pray for you?"

"Yes, just as long as nobody touches me."

Frank prayed for what seemed an hour. Then I got up and left the restaurant.

CHAPTER 10

NEAR THE END

Elijah went before the people and said, "How long will
you waver between two opinions? If the LORD is God,
follow him; but if Baal is God, follow him."

—1 KINGS 18:21

wo days later, I was in Virginia, visiting several customers on the way to the Washington, D.C., area. This area would be the northernmost region worked on this business trip. I would then head southwest and then west until I got home in two weeks. I had fifty customers to visit along the way. Each customer had issues pertaining to the doors they had purchased at one of many retail outlets. I would stop at customers' homes and spend about an hour per visit addressing the typical repair issue.

It was Friday, and I was in the D.C. area, where I had a customer named Bill Wright to visit. My job was to install a new door to replace a defective one he had purchased. We had agreed that I would call him two hours prior to my appointment. When I called, he welcomed me to the area. I noticed that he peppered his sentences with the word "Glory!" I thought, *Oh no. Another Christian. Here we go again . . . This ought to be interesting.* Bill said he might be running late and hoped I would still be at his house when he got home, since he would like to meet me.

I arrived at his house, met his wife and several of his children, and immediately went to work. I was in a hurry to complete the job before Bill got home. I could picture this guy coming and preaching to me, and I didn't want that—not tonight. I was tired. The more I hurried, the more mistakes I made. Normally this job would take three to four hours, but I was well into my fifth hour and running into many issues. I was just about to get the lock installed when behind me I heard "Glory!" I turned. It was Bill.

Bill was a big man. He just stood there smiling at me. He said, "Praise God, the door looks great!" I thanked him and told him I would be done soon. He asked me if I was a Christian, and I said no. He talked to his children for the hour or so it took me to finish my project. He stood behind me every few minutes as he passed the front door to chat about God. I was ready to leave.

He asked me to stay and eat dinner with his family. I was hungry and decided to stay. We sat at a table that could fit twenty people. Bill, his wife, and their seven children sat down and joined hands around the table. Bill began to pray like I had never heard before. He had such a passion. He prayed for me and each one at the table. Then he blessed the food and we ate. Dinnertime was filled with discussions of the children's schoolwork, upcoming family events, and God. After about thirty minutes, dinner was over. I sprang to my feet after we ate, thanked them, and headed for the door.

As I was saying my good-byes, Bill came to me and told me that his family had a custom he would like me to observe: he and his family prayed for everyone who entered their home. I told him, "Thank you, that would be fine," as I was leaving. He said, "No, I mean right now." I reluctantly turned and stood in his foyer as his wife and six of his children walked up to me.

His little girl Lisa, who was about eleven years old, came up to me and put her hand on my shoulder as they prayed. His wife held a three-year-old girl. This girl reached over and put her hand on my heart. Her lips moved as if she were much older and in prayer. The whole family prayed for a long time. I actually felt very weak.

I was walking toward my truck in a daze when Bill came up behind me and startled me. He told me he was on his way to a men's retreat and invited me to join him. The retreat was in the southern Virginia hills in an old Civil War–era hospital turned Catholic retreat compound. He told me he belonged to an Ecumenical Charismatic Catholic church. I wondered what that was. I knew I disliked Catholics mostly because that was the church I grew up in and remembered bad experiences there. The *ecumenical* and *charismatic* part just sounded weird to me. Those terms represented to me those outwardly bold Christians who couldn't fight their way out of a spiritual paper sack—the kind of people who wore cross necklaces, WWJD bracelets, and Christian T-shirts to scare off their greatest fear: Satan, and the real power of the knowledge they hide from.

Bill gave me a map to the men's retreat and told me that if I was anywhere close I would be welcome there as his invited guest. My mind wandered and I thought, *Since we already exchanged phone numbers to arrange our work schedules to fix his door, he is going to call me. I know it; he's going to call me with more "Glory!" and "Glory!" What's up with this guy and glory?*

Bill continued our conversation and told me it wasn't typical to invite anyone who wasn't already signed up because space was limited. His daughter Lisa came outside and, overhearing some of the conversation, told me I should go. I was starting to feel comfortable around Lisa. She reminded me of my youngest daughter, Kristin, when she was that age—tiny build, freckles, cute as can be, tender, and bold. This little evangelist was a bundle of innocence and purity. She was so on fire for her God. It seemed to draw me in some.

I spent that night in a hotel after repairing a couple of doors in the same area. The next morning, I input the next few days' orders in my GPS and headed south. On Saturday, I had only two easy repairs to make in southwest Virginia. After a couple of hours driving, I stopped and completed my first job. The second repair was only three miles away. After I stopped to get a bite to eat, I called the customer, went by, and fixed the door issue he was having in a matter of minutes. It was only 10 a.m., and I had completed what I had scheduled for the day.

I sat in the parking lot of a grocery store to input the rest of my repair orders and make a few calls to customers to schedule work. The customers in the area were not at home or willing to have me work the next day, which was Sunday. Instead I worked on paperwork and organized the truck for about an hour. When I got out of the truck to stretch and go in the store for supplies, a piece of paper fell out and blew a few feet from me. It was the note from Bill with the directions to the retreat. He had also written on the note that he would love for me to stop by.

I noticed I was only six miles from where the men were meeting.

During this period in my life, I was increasingly seeking something I felt I lacked—spiritual stuff, perhaps knowledge I didn't have. I knew I was missing something. I knew I was tired of the life I lived: the hate, the negative thoughts, the lack of feeling love, the numbness and aimlessness. But in addition to the addiction to blood and power, the uncertainty of what would happen if I left satanism after practicing it the past twenty years or so held me in bondage.

I sensed an incredible battle I just did not have the energy to fight without help. I had never experienced real power as I had in the dark arts, and turning away from that would be excruciatingly hard—who was going to step up to the plate and help? I had never seen such power on the "light" side or from the thousands of Christians I encountered. Most of the believers seemed to live in fear.

I had the time, but I did not want to face the fight that would be inevitable if I went to the retreat. Typically, if I was around such men or Christians in general for an extended period of time, I became very unsettled, and a war raged in my spirit. Although I wanted what they had in peace and happiness, the war that existed in and around me was so exhausting it would make me sleep for a day or so afterward. I would be compelled to sleep; and I was a long way from home, with a lot of work to complete before I got there. I just did not have the time. I couldn't imagine what doors would be opened spiritually. I had way too much work to do to contend with the spiritual conflict that came with fraternizing with the other side.

I drove from the parking lot of the store westward toward where the men were meeting. It didn't take long to find the retreat center located in the Virginia hills. I drove to where Bill said he would be and circled a couple of times. Too nervous to go inside, I drove about three miles away to an empty church parking lot and sat staring out the windshield. My phone rang; the caller ID showed Bill Wright's home number. I answered, and little Lisa Wright asked if I was going to the retreat. I told her that I had driven by and felt a little uneasy and was not certain if I had the time with my schedule.

Lisa urged, "Just go there, Mr. Leehan. All the guys are expecting you, and Dad just called to ask me if I had heard from you. He really wants you to stop in." I told her I was unsure, and she again said, "Just go!"

I turned around and headed back to the retreat center. This time, I parked in a field on the backside of the property and again stared out the windshield, feeling numb and alone.

I noticed six main buildings that encompassed the area. They were all the same. Each was about two hundred feet long, two stories high, and about forty feet wide. The eight-inch lap cedar siding was painted white on all the structures. All had green asphalt roof shingles. Windows were evenly placed on both stories, on top of one another and about ten feet apart. These structures were used as sleeping quarters for guests who came to visit the retreat area.

One main building had been a Civil War hospital. Similar to the other buildings, it was twenty or so feet wider than the others. This building now housed the massive kitchen, many meeting rooms, and gathering areas with large windowed foyers, a great place to sit and look outdoors and possibly reflect on the beautiful mountainsides, fall-colored leaves, and wildlife that ventured by. Nestled in the hills of southern Virginia, the retreat area was surrounded on the west and south sides by the Blue Ridge Mountains. I could hear the sounds of vehicles as they slowly made their way down the crushed-rock roads to and from the large retreat center.

Still sitting in my car and focused on a nearby hillside, I started channeling. I lost all sense of reality. I saw a war in the spirit, a major conflict around me everywhere. I witnessed fighting between supernatural beings. Their bodies were not defined, but were light and dark images. I inherently knew what was transpiring. The action was increasingly violent.

Then I was startled by a loud noise. Bill was knocking on the door and looking through the driver's-side window to see if I was okay. I immediately opened the door and greeted him.

I stepped out of the truck in a daze and followed Bill to a small building where praise and worship had just begun with about fifty men in attendance. I sheepishly walked into the room with Bill. Although I was very nervous, I followed his lead and we found a place to stand among the other men.

As long as I could remember, and possibly since childhood, I had a vision that came repeatedly through periods in my life. I saw myself in the sling portion of a slingshot. The bands were pulled back as far as they could go without snapping. My eyes were closed. The place where the band was pulled felt very chaotic. I felt nervous and alone. At any moment I could be released and flung eventually through the axis of the bow of the slingshot. Once I crossed over, I would be safe and secure and propelled into some mission I was unaware of.

I had no idea how to be released from the grip that held tightly on to the sling. I felt as if I had always been in that position. Being in the slingshot was familiar and almost home for me. Yet, if I could ever cross the space between the bow, I felt I could be free of whatever held on to me for so long.

Watching the men praise and worship God, my thoughts were racing. *Is there any way of release, or am I stuck forever in this dark place? Why am I in this dark lifestyle? What did I do to get here? Can I resist and be let go? Can I fight? Is there anyone who can help me escape from this evil lifestyle? Is there anyone who has the stamina to fight for me? Does anyone know how to help me?*

I looked at Bill. He sang and clapped his hands with a big smile on his face as a couple of men led worship and played their acoustic guitars. He glanced at me and said, "Glory!" I was tempted to leave but stayed where I was and closed my eyes.

The longer I stayed, the more at ease I became. I was curious as to why I felt relief from the spiritual battle raging inside me—the first time I had ever felt relief in a church setting. And suddenly I realized, *Wait, I am in praise and worship, and for the first time I am okay and not getting ill or anxious or nervous or angry. What's going on? Why here? Why now?* I felt as if a load was being lifted from my head and shoulders. My thoughts became clearer. It was as if I could breathe easier; my chest felt lighter.

But the darkness wasn't letting go of me that easily. In a matter of minutes, I had a sense of urgency to leave. I was anxious and torn. My stomach churned with a nervous energy. I walked through the door to get outside and stood alongside the building, trying to capture the thoughts that were starting to overwhelm me. I wondered if I could ever be like those men, if I could ever truly be shot out of the slingshot and live without fear. I wanted what they had but didn't know how to get there.

But no matter how much I wanted to be free, there was just too much of the past, too much evil, and too much pain and hurt to let go of to be like them. The confidence I exhibited in their midst was a defense mechanism to thwart any of their further attempts at digging into my life and learning who I really was. No one understood where I had been or where I was.

I trusted no one, especially their God. I always had my guard up. I was always suspicious of the motives of others. Paranoia was constant. Oh yes, there were small breakthroughs from time to time, but I was like a scared and cornered animal looking for an escape route.

After the service, I retreated to my truck.

Exhausted from the spiritual battle, I stayed the night in the truck with the music playing softly in the background. I was invited to sleep in one of the cabins with the men but declined. My truck was a warm and safe place for me. There, I was in control.

The next morning I awoke and looked out the truck's window. I had forgotten where I was. The dew was heavy on the grass. A low-lying fog blanketed the nearby hills. The trees gently swayed to the light easterly breeze that swept through the area. Chilly air hit me as I left the warmth of the cab and walked outside. The sun was very low on the horizon, just now forcing out the darkness.

I walked toward one of the smaller buildings to use the restroom. The smell of bacon cooking permeated the air. Men were walking around to exercise and talk after a long night's sleep. A few were reading papers on the small porches of the cabins where they stayed. Several said hello as I passed. Peace was in this place. I was beginning to feel comfortable now. I didn't feel the pressure of the night before. Although last evening was calming in many ways, it was also conflicting for me; I was torn between two completely different worlds.

As I left the outside latrine, one of Bill's friends stopped me to say hello and said he was glad I was here with the group of men. Minutes later, one of the cooks stuck his head outside the kitchen door and invited us to be one of the first waves of men to eat. Brandon and I joined each other inside the dining area and ate breakfast together. We made small talk about life, relationships, and college football.

After breakfast, I decided to hit the road once again to continue my work. I chose not to stay for worship service. Although peaceful, this place exposed my double-minded spiritual life. I was living between two extremes and did not know which way to turn. I didn't want to be bound in Satan's darkness, but I also didn't feel I could live the way I needed to in order to be a real Christian. I was dancing precariously on top of a narrow wire, and I was teetering. I couldn't maintain my balance in this spot. I knew I was missing something, but I didn't know what that something was. I was stuck on a spiritual high-wire, high above a huge audience of onlookers, with no net to catch me if I fell.

By midmorning, with the retreat center far behind me, I was off and running once again. I turned my truck south and continued my busy schedule. I had gained some orders while on the road and had another sixty or so jobs strewn about on my way back to Oklahoma. It would take me a couple of weeks to make it home.

In three days' time, I had stopped in Pennsylvania and upper Maryland and completed fifteen or so jobs and made my way to Ohio. The time behind the wheel gave me ample opportunity to evaluate my time with the guys last weekend and the life I had known the last twenty years. The temporary peace I felt at the retreat gradually subsided. I started feeling as I had for so long; I retreated in my thoughts to my familiar lifestyle and to the dark spirits I had known so well. I wasn't sure why, but in this moment I didn't feel punished for collaborating with "the other side." Nothing happened to me other than my dismissing the past weekend as a fluke.

As the memories of the weekend and the guys faded, so did the glint of hope I momentarily felt that life could be normal for me. I was different and had a chosen path.

✛

It was another Wednesday evening, and I once again began to feel driven to fulfill the longtime assignment that had been given to me—to disrupt another church service and pass out diabolical bibles. It was like another force took over the steering wheel of my truck. As I sat in the cab, I looked out the windshield to discover I was in the parking lot of a medium-sized Baptist church. (This was one of my favorite denominations to mess with.)

I had three satanic bibles to distribute. I stuffed the bibles in my sweatshirt and exited my truck. People were making their way to the church before the services started. Several glanced at me and said hello. I hadn't slept much in the past couple of days and hadn't shaven. I looked rough. I made my way to the church doors and stopped before entering. I looked in through the doors and saw smiling faces. I heard the congregation singing a song about a "rugged cross"; I did not like that song.

It took all the strength I had, but I resisted my assignment to distribute the satanic bibles, walked off the steps of the church, and jumped into the cab of my truck.

I sat in the truck and immediately suffered a severe headache. I started sweating and became very anxious. I started the engine, and as the truck idled, I closed my eyes and remembered the men at the retreat just days earlier. I thought of their demeanor, their gentleness, their kindness and love. The more I thought, the more intense the battle within me became. I fought the impulses for probably the first time in my life. I looked down to see that my right wrist had a superficial cut on it and was seeping blood.

As blood dripped from my wrist, I emerged from the truck with the rest of the bibles in my hand. The pages of several of the books had blood droplets on them. I pulled a cigar from my shirt pocket and lit it as I walked toward the back of the church property. I sat unnoticed on the curb of the rear parking lot. As I gazed into the distant night, I pulled the lighter from my pocket and caught a corner of one of the bibles on fire. I placed the rest of the bibles on top of the blaze and simply walked away.

I became physically ill as I got to the truck. I was sweating heavily. I pulled my shirt over my head and threw it to the ground. The crisp air cooled my body as it penetrated my skin. I sat next to my truck, tilted my head back as I looked into the starlit sky, and tried to compose myself. I threw up violently twice. I picked up my shirt, wiped my mouth with it, started the truck, and drove away.

I drove for a couple of hours to northern Ohio and pulled into a truck stop. The night was very rough for me. I could not sleep and was plagued with nightmares and night sweats. As the hours passed that night, I became more unsettled. I had been rebelling against my instincts and was presently paying a heavy price.

I left the truck at 3 a.m. and walked down the street to a nearby Denny's restaurant. With temperatures in the upper thirties, I had my usual jeans on but only a T-shirt to shield my upper body from the cold. I didn't feel the elements and insisted to the waiter that I wanted to sit on the outside patio. I sat and drank a pot of coffee in the hours before dawn. I stared into the dark sky and hoped with all that was in me that my life could change. I was emotionally exhausted and physically tired.

I continued to work in Ohio for the following three days. The rest of the trip was more subdued than the early part of this trip or any other I had made. I was more self-controlled and less apt to want to create havoc somewhere. It is hard to explain, but I felt something I never had.

The day after I got home, I was sitting in my office at work. I thought a lot that day. The business was in total disarray. My relationship with Maggie was over. We were still living together, but only due to personal and business financial concerns. It had been a very trying day at the office. I had to let go of a couple of employees due to loss of business. The company revenues were in the negative monthly, and all signs indicated that within a few weeks my firm would have to close its doors for good. A call came from the gentleman from whom we leased our building. He demanded payment immediately. We were in arrears two months in our rental agreement. I got off the phone with my company's landlord and went home.

When I arrived at the house, Maggie was in her office, on the phone with a friend. I stuck my head in to say hello, and she nodded. I went into the backyard to rake some leaves and do some busywork. My body was in the backyard doing physical labor, but my mind was far away. I was recalling all the family times in this house. I was recalling all the fun times, the evil times, and the in-between times—so many experiences. We had lived here six years. I felt deep inside that I had been dancing on the proverbial fence for so long. I had been dancing, and now it was time to pay the fiddler.

Deep in thought, my spirit torn, I felt very heavy and ill with worry and fret. My anxiety level was high. I did not know how I could go on another day. I saw no hope or resolution with all the problems that were on my doorstep. The devil himself was on the threshold of my life, saying to me, *"It is time."* Now, this wasn't like the voice I heard when I was above the ambulance. That one had a peace to it. This voice I knew well. It was a familiar tone, low and alluring. This voice inspired fear, total terror. I felt my lord was with me, and there was no way out. Complete hopelessness invaded my spirit.

Maggie got off the phone and walked up to me with a question that should have been asked long ago, a question that divided the spiritual realm. She wore a solemn look, with resolution and finality in her appearance. She had possibly come to a conclusion as to what I would say and what her action would be to my answer.

She said, "Mike, I need to ask you something. I need you to think about it before you answer. But before you do, I want to tell you that I will always love you. I care for you and just want you to know that. You need to think before you respond."

I said, "Oh no. No matter what I say, I know my life is about to change."

She just looked at me. I could tell she was hurting deeply. Her spirit was burdened. She finally asked, "Is Jesus your Lord? Can you profess His name and tell me He is your Savior?"

I knew what my response should be to comfort her. I knew what I needed to say. I knew that the consequences of my response would affect my world in a major way. My thoughts went through every possible scenario from any answer I could give. I quickly thought of how I could manipulate the situation, how I could skirt the issue and not be forced to expose the underlying cesspool of thought and lifestyle. I had been with her twelve years—why would this question come up now?

I searched all possibilities as I started to answer her. But out of my mouth came the only answer I could reply with: "No."

The truth of my answer astounded even me. The question she asked carried the weight of the world in it. The answer divides people and peoples, creates wars, and in many cases, leads to death. My answer was true. Why did I choose not to lie? I am not certain. My father was the father of lies. It was out of my heart, and was a relief not to hide it from anyone any longer.

Her response was candid. She said, "The kids and I are going to move out."

Maggie had already found a home that she liked. I had gone with her looking at houses the past several weeks. I knew we would be moving since we were behind on house payments, and at the time, I thought we would be moving together. Her thoughts were quite different. It didn't matter what the outcome. I simply answered that I would be glad to help move her and her children.

For the next month, I helped Maggie ready the house she had purchased. It was a nice home in an established neighborhood in town. Quite a bit of work was needed to prepare the house for us to move in. Electrical work and painting needed to be completed before furniture could be moved in. Basic carpentry work had to be done to update the house. I installed a security and surveillance system. I ran a computer network throughout the house. I installed new doors.

It took a week to move Maggie's and the kids' personal belongings to the new house. All of the furniture, pictures, accessories, and signs of life were out of the home we once lived in together.

I was alone. A single mattress lay on the floor of the master bedroom. The house was void of liveliness and love, cold and empty, a great physical and emotional loss. The spiritual covering that had once been on the house due to Maggie's prayers and presence was gone. The property was now completely open to the stealthy forces that were waiting to emerge from beneath its foundation.

Each day I remained, the more intense the spiritual battle became. The nights were full of terror and lack of sleep. The days were full of disappointment and hard physical labor. I was not only losing my home to foreclosure; I was also forced to move out of my offices due to lack of revenue to make the lease payments. My world was collapsing around me. For three weeks I emptied the warehouse and office space into a couple of rented storage units. Most of what was left in the business and home was not worth moving, but it was all I had left. At this point, I didn't care much; I was prepping myself for an end to my existence.

One late night, I was very tired, and I didn't know how much more I could stand of the pressures in life I was facing. At 11 p.m., I decided to turn out the lights and lie down. About twenty minutes later, I heard something in the kitchen. It sounded as if someone were coughing. Then I heard several people talking. I couldn't tell what was being said, since they were whispering. I lay still in the dark, trying to determine who they were and how they got into the house. I assumed it may have been Maggie or some of my kids checking in on me.

As I stayed still on the mattress, I felt heaviness on top of me, as if a large person were sitting on my chest. I could hardly breathe, and each breath was labored. I could not move my body other than my right hand. All I could do was look down toward my feet. I held my phone in my right hand and began to text the last person I had talked to, Chris Spradlin, the Oklahoma City LifeChurch campus pastor. I texted Chris that I needed help at my house; that was all I could get written before the pressure increased on top of me. He responded that he would be there in thirty minutes. This would be the longest thirty minutes of my life.

The moment I thought it couldn't get worse, it did. I heard the footsteps of several people coming down the long hallway. Each step was slow and deliberate. The wooden floors creaked from the weight on them, and it sounded like an army of soldiers marching toward the bedroom. I could not move. The noises became more intense with a low-level chanting that accompanied the footsteps. Never in my life had I experienced such fear. The chanting in the hall grew louder the closer the footsteps came to the bedroom.

I could not look around as I lay still. The pressure on top of me was still present but had lightened enough to allow me to breathe. I heard the steps on the wooden floor subside as they transitioned onto the carpet of the bedroom. Slowly I heard their advancement toward my mattress on the far side of the room. At a systematic pace they came toward me. My eyes were fixed open when I heard the chanting stop. I could not look behind me but felt a nudge on the front of the mattress beneath my head. My breath left my body, and I gasped for air.

Silence was broken only by the sound of the wood crackling as it burned in the fireplace. The flames moved violently as a wind swept through the room. Outside the patio door that was directly to my right, I caught a glimpse of two raccoons peering in the window. I felt a cold breath of air being forced into my mouth. The air expanded my chest as it entered. The coldness of it left a burning sensation in my mouth, throat, and lungs. My stomach began to growl as if I hadn't eaten in days. I became very chilled. Then I heard a loud knock at the door and felt the darkness over my body back away.

The heavy presence lifted enough that I could ease my struggling body to its feet. I stumbled out of the bedroom and made my way to the door. Chris Spradlin and Chris Beall (campus pastors), John Zeigler (local police officer and head of security at our church), and another man (to whom I was not introduced) came for spiritual support and to pray with the others. They were a welcome sight to my sore eyes; I was exhausted. All fight in me was extinguished. Nothing was left.

"Come on in," I said to the men.

Chris Spradlin was first in the house and immediately said, "What's going on, Mike? You look wiped out!"

As I ushered them in, we walked from the living room area to the master bedroom in silence. It had to be an eerie feeling for the men. I couldn't say a word at that moment as I was trying to gather my thoughts.

"Thanks for coming, guys," I said.

I sat on the floor with my back against a wall, John Zeigler stood against yet another wall, and Chris Spradlin and Chris Beall sat down near me. The other gentleman stood with Zeigler. After a big sigh, Chris Spradlin said, "Tell me what is going on."

"I don't know if I can carry on. Some stuff just happened here that was unbelievable."

"Mike, your whole story is unbelievable, dude," Spradlin said.

I looked up, and I saw Chris Beall with his eyes closed and his hands up close to his face as if he were praying.

"I hear ya, but it seems as if everything is amping up a bit," I countered.

Chris Spradlin continued, "So what the heck happened? Talk to me."

"I heard this chanting come down the hall, and heavy footsteps. The footsteps stopped when the mattress over there, which I was lying on, was bumped. Then it was as if cold air were forced through my mouth. I couldn't move; there was something very heavy holding me down. I tried to close my eyes but could not. I couldn't breathe; then I heard you guys knock on the door."

Chris Beall then said, "Mike, I have never felt such a heaviness as I feel in this house."

Zeigler and the other man looked on intently.

"Dude, we need to pray," Chris Spradlin blurted out.

After Spradlin prayed, he asked, "What are you going to do?"

I answered, "Not sure, but here." I handed him a 9mm bullet that I had originally intended for Craig Groeschel. But since that plan was thwarted, I had decided to use that bullet on me. I was shaking as I handed over what I called the "magic bullet"—the one I had marked with a magic marker several months prior to loading it in the clip the day I intended to use it on Craig. Spradlin held the bullet in his hand, staring at it for a moment, and said, "Wow, this is it, huh?"

I looked him in the eye, nodded my head, and said, "Yes."

The room went silent for a moment. Then Chris Beall said, "Mike, I am concerned about you being here. I have never felt such heaviness and oppression. This is absolutely unbearable. I really think you need to get out of here and not look back. Do you have somewhere to stay tonight?"

I eased out the words, "I do."

Chris Spradlin looked at me with deep concern and said, "I

can't stand this heaviness anymore. What do you say we all get out of here!"

We all walked from the master bedroom and through the house and garage to the driveway. The four men couldn't get to their cars fast enough. Chris Beall was the closest to me and said, "Mike, you are leaving, right? You have to get away from here!"

"Yeah, Chris, if your cars were not behind me, I would already be gone," I said.

He came back with, "What about your clothes and such?"

I answered, "I will come back tomorrow in the light of day and get what little I have left."

As Chris Beall jumped into the van, Chris Spradlin interjected, "Mike, I know God has this whole thing worked out. Just hang in there and do not give up."

"I will try not to," I said weakly.

As their cars backed out of the driveway and headed down the street, I jumped in my truck and was close behind them.

The evening's occurrence alerted me to the danger I was in. Satan overplayed his hand, and I finally picked up on it. I knew the darkness I was involved in could eventually catch up with me, but I always thought I had an upper hand and could manipulate those who manipulated me. I was wrong. Satan had me convinced I was more quick-witted, cleverer, and a step ahead of authorities and those in my life. I needed help, and I needed it quickly.

The next day I picked up what little I had left at the property. I never returned.

CHAPTER 11

NOWHERE TO RUN,
NOWHERE TO HIDE

This day I call the heavens and the earth as witnesses against you that I have set before you life and death, blessings and curses. Now choose life, so that you and your children may live.

—DEUTERONOMY 30:19

I left the house on Oak Creek Drive and the mayhem that existed there, and within two days, I moved to a condo that Maggie owned. The condo's previous tenants had just purchased their own home and relocated. Timing was perfect for my moving in. The condo was one-third the size of the house on Oak Creek Drive but was pleasant and provided a roof over my head.

The neighborhood was primarily full of retirees and college students from the nearby University of Central Oklahoma. This seemed as though it would be a quiet place to live.

My daughter Marisa lived in her own home in a nearby neighborhood within walking distance. That provided me a chance to spend occasional time with her and my two granddaughters.

I thought that perhaps when I left my home on Oak Creek Drive, some of the supernatural manifestations and weird stuff would subside. This didn't happen; nighttime noises, visitations, and terror continued.

One late night, I was in bed and heard talking downstairs. I left the warmth of bed to see if I had left a TV on in the living room. Walking downstairs, I looked over the edge of the banister, and the television was off. Still hearing the muffled sounds of low-level conversation, I went into the downstairs bedroom to investigate. It was obvious the talking was coming from this room. However, I didn't see anyone. I ventured farther into the room and to the closed walk-in closet door. I located the source of the sound; it was coming from the closet.

When I opened the door I was stunned to see three figures in a faded appearance standing in the corner of the closet, dressed in black formal attire with red ties—I knew at once that they were spirits. This was the first time I had seen spirits in this form; always before they were shadows that spoke, or I simply knew they were there and could feel their presence. During ritual times, these shadows would enter my body. I knew people who had seen demons visually, and I had read about occurrences where demons would appear, but I had been content in the form that they communicated with me. I did not need to see a physical form to be convinced they existed. I knew they did.

One of them said, *"I don't think he can see us."* Another one said, *"I think he still has the ability."* The other just watched and scratched his head. I thought, *Too much is going on in my life. If I communicate with them, it could open some doors. I better just leave. Man, am I sick of this stuff. Wonder why they are so bold as to appear to me? They are coming for me . . .*

I acted as if I had come to the closet for a winter coat and selected one from a hanger, ignoring the threesome. I closed the door behind me as I left the closet and didn't stop as I left the bedroom. The hair on the back of my neck was standing up. Without shoes on and just wearing my winter pajamas and now a winter coat, I left the house. I was exhausted.

I drove off in my truck. I wondered why the figures were in my closet. I drove around town for a bit to sort things out in my mind.

Returning home a couple of hours later, I walked straight upstairs and crawled into my warm bed and retired for the evening. No other encounter happened that evening. I slept through the night and continued on the next day as if last night's incident had never occurred. You see, that was my way to handle certain circumstances in my life, even one this extraordinary. This was not a battle I was going to confront in my life at this time; not this day. As weird as it was, I'd had weirder and stranger, and I quite simply wasn't going to address it.

In the condo, the dark spiritual activity escalated and even manifested with physical evidence. I wasn't the only resident who occupied this space. The closet incident was not the only one in which I encountered visitors in this house. Nighttime was filled with many sounds: chairs moving on the tile floor, the opening and closing of cabinet doors, and the cold air blowing through the house from a previously locked front door left mysteriously open in the wee hours of morning. I would get up and investigate from time to time, but after it became normal to have bizarre happenstance around me for so long, I would ignore it and fall back to sleep.

At times, I woke to a crushing weight on my chest, to the bed moving, or from having my blankets torn off of me and thrown to the floor. Occasionally, a lamp would turn off and on, the water in the shower would run full steam, or the patio door would slide open. Most often I tried to ignore the intrusions, but occasionally

I would just turn the shower off, pick up a lamp, or close a door and return to sleep. When in the not-so-distant past I would be intrigued and delve into communication with them, at this juncture, I fought that impulse and figured if I ignored them, they would go elsewhere. I became accustomed to others being around and making their presence known. A couple of things I did realize: we are not alone in our little biospheres—and we really never have complete privacy. Someone or something is always peering into the minute world of our experience.

After years of seeking and experiencing spiritual prowess and knowledge, it became apparent to me that we are truly spirit beings just on this earth for a short season. The spiritual world was real to me and at times much more real than the physical world in which I lived. I knew with certainty the spirit realm was more alive and active than the world I was born into. I sensed that we as humans were actually not much different from pet fish—someone (or something) is always peering in to check us out. Only in our case, spirit beings interact with us much more than we do with our aquatic pets. They can enter into our environment and change the path we are on.

†

Despite the escalating demonic activity in my home (or perhaps because of it), my spiritual life was changing. The dark had lost its luster. I was no longer intrigued by the darkness, hungry for its power. Instead, I was looking for some relief, hoping to experience some of the spiritual light I had glimpsed in others.

Venturing to LifeChurch campuses during the next several months became common. It was an issue of survival. The more driven I had become to learn about God, the more the dark spiritual activity at the condo increased. Something had to go.

I began to think about killing myself so that the battle would be over, or would it end there? That was the prevailing thought in my life. Some might ask whether the thought of hell scared me. The answer is no. I had truly gotten to a point that if the existence of hell was real, then it wasn't relevant to me; I didn't care. The depictions of hell I had heard about were just goofy horror stories anyway. In some sick and twisted way, the torments and visitations I had in my actual life "scared the hell *out of me*." I was no longer scared of a place that may or may not actually exist.

As early November 2007 weather turned cold, my internal war grew more intense. I continued visiting church on Sundays and attending the Damascus Men's group on Monday evenings. I also continued with the Wednesday night Bible studies at Kristie's home. On the inside, I was lost, hopeless, without direction, and certain I was the one soul who was beyond the reach of God. I felt hopeless, adrift in a sea of unforgivable sin, lost and abandoned without love.

My nights were horrid, filled with nightmares and visions of death. I seldom slept, and the fatigue, coupled with the chronic depression from seeking a God who seemed unreachable, left me exhausted. As the weeks passed, I fell into deeper depression, and with Christmas approaching, the feelings intensified. I had quit doing my carpentry jobs well over three weeks earlier and had no income, but why would I need it? I was at my end, and I knew it. In fact, I resolved that this Christmas would be my last. I couldn't take much more.

After the holidays, I sat alone in a dark corner of my living room and spiritually saw that January 13 would be the day of my death. Just as I was directed to kill Craig Groeschel, the same spirit came to me this night and told me that January 13 would be my time. I had failed in my assignment with Craig. I was being called home to an eternity of darkness.

When I received this morbid news, all I felt was relief that this battle would soon be over. Good, bad, or indifferent, I had accepted the idea that no matter what lay ahead in the afterlife, I was ready for it. I was done with the drudgery of this existence, and I just wanted relief. I was less frightened of an uncertain afterlife than I was the hellish life I was leading. I couldn't take it any longer.

After my decision, I experienced an uptick in mood. The days were easier. I began counting down the days to January 13. Only a few more days to freedom, and this world and its troubles would be a dead memory. I didn't utter a word to anyone about my plans.

At this same time, my good friend, mentor, and counselor, Bob Sanders, was in a hospice care facility, suffering from the effects of cancer. Bob had been in the hospital a while and had been battling his illness for nearly a year. Bob had been a positive influence in my life for the past fifteen years. My heart hurt for him and his family, but I didn't know how to react to them.

One night, Maggie and I went to visit Bob at the hospice facility. Bob's younger son, Brian, was there. We stayed awhile, speaking to Brian while Bob slept. At this stage in his illness, Bob was rarely awake.

I walked into Bob's room alone and sat next to him. He was asleep, but I talked to him anyway. If I could have cried while I spoke to him, I would have. I was close to Bob and didn't want him to leave this world. I had subdued my feelings and tears for so long, I couldn't express my emotions. My heart was hardened by my past, and I hadn't cried in forty-five years. I said, "Bob, I know you are asleep, but I wanted to tell you I have been going to church. I really am seeking God. I am going to a couple of Bible studies and with all my heart want God in my life. I haven't found Him yet, but I am earnestly seeking."

I went on talking to Bob as if he were sitting up in a chair and totally coherent. I told him how bad I had been, my wrongs, and how I hoped I could be forgiven. I told him I was even considering going to an upcoming Christian men's retreat with the Damascus Men. I told him I had an issue, though: I didn't know if I could keep strong enough for the inevitable battle. I told him I wished I would just die and get it over with. I told him I missed our talks and coffees together. My heart started really hurting as he lay there. I didn't know how to handle the pain. I thought of my dad's death and his funeral; the moment brought up memories of relationship break-ups, times when separated from my children, loneliness, and such things. I didn't know how to handle emotional pain; I just bottled it up and tucked it away in the dark recesses of my mind.

After a few minutes of this one-sided conversation, I stood up from the chair to leave the room. Bob never opened his eyes but started speaking, which startled me. He said, "Where are you going?" He went on to tell me he knew not only that I had been seeking God earnestly but that I would finally be one with the Lord and would accept Christ as my Savior. He said it so confidently, as if he really did know. He said it as if he had had a talk with God and God had confided in him that his friend Michael would be okay.

Bob, in a quiet voice, said, "Michael, I know you will find the Lord. I know you will be okay. So will I."

I turned back to speak to him, and he had fallen asleep. I left the room, and shortly thereafter Bob died.

Although I was too emotionally hardened to grieve at the time, I knew I would miss Bob. I would miss our talks in local coffee shops and restaurants where we discussed life's issues and mental health. I didn't quite understand Bob's faith and all his talk about God's love and grace, but I knew that Bob cared for me. He was more than just a friend to me; he was the godly father I didn't have.

✝

Sunday came, and I joined Maggie at church. We did our usual routine: she went in, and I stayed in the foyer. Craig started his sermon. It was all familiar now: four songs, a video clip, a timed or recorded sermon, altar call, video, dismissal. Everything was choreographed, perfected through trial and error. The goal was to lead those in attendance who may not be saved to raise their hands and accept Christ into their lives, the first step. I heard the message clearly through the TV monitors, but I did not make a commitment. For the first time, my hand almost raised involuntarily in an attempt, I suppose, at self-preservation. A part of me was ready to surrender to Christ's control. However, another part of me rebelled and refused to submit.

As soon as church was over, I went to the condo and fell asleep. I woke the following day, what was to be my last Monday on earth, and it was appropriately cloudy and cold. No need to get out of bed. I returned to the warmth under the heavy comforter and fell into a deep, dark slumber.

When I woke it was 6 p.m. I had slept away another day, and after a few minutes of collecting my thoughts, realized that the Damascus Men's group would be starting in forty minutes or so. But I didn't want to leave the cocoon I had made for myself the past two days. I wasn't going to the men's group. Why would it matter anyway?

CHAPTER 12

FROM DARKNESS TO LIGHT

Now get up and stand on your feet. I have appeared to
you to appoint you as a servant and as a witness of what
you have seen and will see of me. I will rescue you from
your own people and from the Gentiles. I am sending you
to them to open their eyes and turn them from darkness
to light, and from the power of Satan to God.

—ACTS 26:16–18

Once January 13 became the settled day of my departure, I began to take stock of the shambles my life had become. The business I'd built up from nothing and poured my heart into over the past eight years was gone. My twelve-year relationship with Maggie had ended. Aside from a brief visit with my mother, I had had no contact with my biological family (except my children) for four years. I was unemployed and had legal problems that would overwhelm a seasoned attorney. I was broke, and had no direction, no hope, and seemingly no reason to live. I'd hit bottom.

I wrote suicide notes to my children and to a few other people. I contemplated the best method to end my life. A bullet through the temple seemed logical and efficient, but after a little more thought, the picture of my traumatized children standing over my bloody remains caused me to reconsider. *Okay*, I thought, *I'll hang myself.* I guess the idea of my body gently swaying in a light breeze seemed better than lying in a pool of blood. I decided to string a length of rope with a noose around the top floor rear deck and end my life that way.

I came home from a small carpentry job I was doing for an elderly woman to a freezing house due to an unpaid gas bill. The temperature in the house was further affected by the cold, palpable, spiritual presence that surrounded me.

For some reason, cleaning the house before hanging myself seemed like a good idea, and I began to clean and disinfect. Picking up clutter, vacuuming, and dusting, I began to feel as if every cell in my body were being sucked out. My spirit sank, my mind went blank, and my energy faded.

I found a twenty-foot section of heavy sisal rope in the garage and dragged the rope upstairs behind me and climbed into bed. I skillfully tied a noose in the rope, then stepped outside onto the patio in a daze and looked over the handrail, making a plan for what would be the last week of my life. This was the eighth of January, a cold and unusually quiet night.

My spirits low, I thought back over my life. I saw a small boy playing alone in a park in the California sunshine; he was, even then, unsure of his place in the world, a boy who was frightened, neglected, and insecure. Then appeared a man who'd failed at marriage and at fatherhood; a man who was closed off emotionally and afraid to love. I saw a man with no intimate friends who was lonely, isolated, and afraid to face the future. These visions washed over me like so many tears. I remember Bob Sanders's words over me as he lay dying and thought, *I'm sorry, Bob, but I guess I cannot be reached after all.*

Wrapping one end of the rope around the base of a four-by-four post and tying several knots to secure the rope, I dropped it from the deck and checked the length. It was too long; I would hit the ground before my neck broke. I untied and restrung the rope. Perfect. The time was inching closer. I was ready to end the pain, the embarrassment, and the suffering. Relief was on its way. Just one more week and I'd be out of this misery.

✝

On the night of January 11, I was in the kitchen, making waffles, when my cell phone rang. Darius was calling to invite me to a retreat the Damascus Men's group had planned for the weekend. He was sincere and at another time might have persuaded me. But I had no intention of spending my last weekend on earth trapped in a cabin with a bunch of touchy-feely God-lovers.

Doing normal activities like cooking and cleaning after a self-imposed death sentence was in a way calming. As I stirred and scrubbed, any lingering fear of death was vanishing into a cloud of mundane and now meaningless tasks.

I began to cook and cook and cook but never ate. I just kept myself busy, and cooking was a way to pass time. It was also an unnoticed symptom of a very serious problem: I wanted isolation. I didn't want to have to interact with another person. Whatever lay ahead of me after January 13 had to be an improvement over this pain-filled, hopeless excuse of a life. I wanted out. So I just continued killing time, before killing myself.

I was cleaning the condo when the phone rang.

"Mike, what are you doing?" Maggie asked.

"Not much, just cleaning."

"Aren't you going to the men's retreat? It's this weekend, right?"

"No, I don't think so. I got other plans. Besides, my truck is on empty, and I don't have gas money. And what the heck would I do there anyway? I just don't fit in with those guys."

"Mike. Listen to me. This is important. You need to be there. I really think this will be a crucial weekend for you!" Maggie sensed my downward spiral and knew I was in a dangerous place.

Maggie insisted I come over so we could talk about this face-to-face. I agreed to go over for a short while. So right in the middle of my cooking, I just left the condo with the stove on, the food out, and the front door wide open. I was like a zombie, consumed by my own depression.

About halfway to Maggie's, my truck ran out of fuel. I pulled into the drive of the nearby National Guard Armory, and my truck sputtered to a stop. Utterly unemotional, I stared out into the night: no anger, no frustration, just numbness. My will to fight was long gone. I'd given up. Maggie called, I told her what had happened, and she soon showed up with a gas can. Surprisingly upbeat, she handed me the gas can and reminded me what a positive experience the retreat could be for me this weekend. She smiled and walked back to the warmth of her car. I looked over at her through her windshield as I poured the fuel into my truck from the can. My mood sank lower.

But then I saw Maggie trying to say something to me. "Just go, just go!" she said emphatically. Despite her persistence, I had no intention of going.

As fate would have it, my truck wouldn't start right away, so Maggie was given more time to urge me to go. By the time it started, she'd convinced me to drive the twenty miles north, where the men were meeting. I agreed—mostly to shut her up, but also for a tank of gas, as she agreed to meet me at a gas station where she'd fill the tank. As soon as the truck was fueled, I went by the house, with Maggie watching my every move, in order to get a few things before going to the men's group. While I packed, Maggie turned off the oven and straightened the kitchen. I am certain after knowing me for twelve years, Maggie sensed a very serious depression in me. She had asked a couple of times if I thought about killing myself, and I answered no. I think she knew that wasn't true.

Once on the road, I pulled over a few times, second-guessing my decision. It was getting late, I was tired, I had a headache, my back hurt, and I was becoming increasingly more nauseous at the prospect of being trapped all weekend with a bunch of guys who wanted nothing more than to just open up with me. With Sunday, January 13, looming, spending Friday and Saturday with the choirboys seemed like such a waste of time. Was this entire Christian neighborly hubbub supposed to be taken seriously? All this happy backslapping and "Love ya, bro" nonsense—was this to play a part in my tragedy? If it wasn't playacting, where did these emotions come from? What would make grown men behave this way?

I thought over the irony of my situation, barely concealing a wry smirk. If any of these guys had an inkling of where I'd been, they'd surely turn and run in terror. How could they possibly understand me? They didn't know the spiritual sewer I'd been swimming in for most of my life. What would they say to someone who'd made a blood oath with the devil? Try slapping a chummy "I understand ya, bro" on that one! These warm-fuzzy Bible men, steeped in wholesome cleanliness and unstained by the darker things of this world—they couldn't possibly see the filthy scars left all over me by evil itself.

They didn't know that I'd conceded my soul to Satan and

that my own personal D-day was coming this Sunday. I contemplated telling them, "Hi, I'm Mike, I'm a satanist, and I'm going to kill myself the day after tomorrow." That's an icebreaker, all right. Strangely relaxed and empowered by such thoughts, I continued driving.

The retreat sat in the middle of a 640-acre tract of land a few miles from the nearest paved road just east of Guthrie, Oklahoma. As I pulled up, my truck began to sputter as though it was out of gas. Had twenty gallons only bought me twenty miles? I coasted to a stop and sat in the truck, not wanting to go in. Nodding off, I was stirred by a voice from the driver's-side window.

"Hey, dude, glad you made it!" Darius greeted me with a big smile.

"Oh, hey," I replied with head and hands slumped over the wheel. I shut my eyes and wished myself into another place, but when I opened them again, there was bright, shiny Darius still looking in at me. I thought he saw a defeated, broken man, and wisely decided not to push.

"Listen, dude, we're all inside, just hanging out. Come on in whenever you're ready. I know everyone will be glad to see you."

Painful words in my ears. But of course he meant well. I sat in the car, gripping the wheel. I breathed deeply and tried to clear the dense fog out of my head. Somehow I mustered the resolve to get out of the truck and walk to the cabin. After being greeted with the expected "hellos" and "how are yous?" I saw a group of men in jeans and tennis shoes, clustered around a TV, watching a movie. The day felt heavy. I just looked for a bed.

"Hey, Mike," the group's leader said, "you gotta come with us into town. We're going to play dodgeball at a local church. Blow off some steam. Fool around for a while. It'll be fun."

The next thing I knew, I was in the back of a van with eight guys trying to talk with me. I had nothing to say, so I sat there, trying to close myself like a heavy front door.

At the gym, I watched the guys running around like kids, laughing and carrying on. I couldn't stand all this lighthearted fun; it made me furious. The last thing I wanted to do was socialize. And their idea of fun seemed so strange to me. *Well, what is "fun"?* I wondered.

I kept myself occupied by filling out a psyche/spiritual personal survey that Jim Kimbrough had given me: a fifteen-page document asking all the standard questions, trying to get at where I had been in life, where I was spiritually, what my beliefs were. Jim was the friend I had met at a Vineyard Bible study when I lived on Abilene Street. Despite the fact that I tried to disrupt his Bible study, Jim still pursued a friendship with me. Unbelievably, he was still trying to show me the love of God. He had given me the spiritual survey a few weeks back, and I happened to have it in my truck, so I brought it with me to the gym.

The survey busied me for the next hour or so, as the men continued to bounce around themselves, playing their games. I watched them from a cold distance. *I'll fill out your survey and listen to you rattle on about your God, but I know what's coming, and no one can stop it.* Their joy seemed so alien to me at that moment. *What a waste of time.*

Back at the cabins, most of the guys sat around and fellowshipped. I found a basement room where mattresses were laid out on the floor. I picked one out and lay down to rest. A few guys tried to come in at various times and talk to me, but I would either ask them to leave or just ignore them. I'm sure I'm not the first person who's ever acted rudely at a church function, but I was convinced I had been the worst one these men ever had to deal with. In spite of my poisonous mood and general standoff-ishness, the men continued to show me nothing but kindness. I wondered if I should feel ashamed.

My sleep was precarious, sometimes marked with a sense of terror, sometimes just restless or fitful. I gnashed my teeth so badly that I broke one. Once, I awoke in a daze and just stared blankly at the ceiling. I waited for dawn amid the sound of men snoring, smacking, grunting, and rolling over in bed; I was com-pletely disgusted.

I got up around 4 a.m. and went outside. Walking in the crisp winter air felt refreshing after being trapped in the "man cave." Within an hour or so, Lynn Seaton, the cook/mentor/sage, put coffee on and made breakfast. Not many of the guys were up yet—most had stayed up late talking, laughing, fellowshipping, and praising.

Once the men finally came to, they picked up right where they left off with more prayer and Bible study. *Do these guys ever give it a break?* I thought. I wandered around, sipped coffee, and stayed as far away from them as I could. After a few hours, they told me they were all going to a nearby field to play gladiator games. I couldn't imagine being in mock combat with these holy warriors. I declined the invitation. The last man made his way to the field, and I was relieved to be alone again.

Compared to how I felt trying to mix with God's "good ol' boys," being alone in my condo sounded better than a trip to the French Riviera. I was miserable, sinking lower and lower. I decided now was the time to make my move. I hurried down-stairs, grabbed my bags, and headed for my truck. I hopped in, thinking this would be an easy, clean break. I turned the ignition.

"Come, on," I pleaded. I tried again. Nothing. I waited and tried again. Same result. I slapped the seat in frustration and considered the options. No way would I consider asking for help and have to listen to one of these Christian handymen sing me a Jesus song while he ran me to the gas station for fuel. How could I be out of gas anyway? I was stuck.

Walking through the woods surrounding the cabins, I fumed and huffed and sent a text message to Maggie: "I am not happy." That message must have raised a red flag in her mind. In the twelve years we'd been together, she'd never seen anything so straightforward from me. This message was direct and simple, with no F-bombs, no lengthy explanation, and no self-absorbed drama. Just "I'm not happy," which to her was an obvious cry for help. She texted back, "Just come home and we can go to church tonight."

Why on earth would I do that? I didn't believe in Christ. I didn't believe there was hope. I'd been in a war, and I was the casualty. I was tired of church, tired of pretending. I was ready to give up.

Trapped someplace I didn't want to be, I got more frustrated by the minute. A violent anger rose inside me. I flew into a rage, kicking the ground and cursing the day I was born. Under a state of what I know now to be extreme satanic oppression, I became more dangerous and unpredictable. When you consider a man who's resigned himself to death by his own hand in less than twenty-four hours, how much could he care about anyone else?

Again, Satan had me isolated and turning inward, convinced that my life would always be this hopeless and unredeemed. I believe wholeheartedly that the underworld was alive with ravenous laughter, aware that the time of my departure, and subsequent arrival in hell, was fast approaching.

A cool gust of morning air cut through me and pulled me back from my outburst and cleared my head enough to think. I'd written notes to my ex-wife, to my children, and to Maggie and her daughters. The only note left to be written was to Maggie's son, Andrew. This would be a tough one. As with every other person who'd crossed my path in this life, I'd never managed to bond with Andrew. He was a great kid with so much going for him, but I just couldn't reach out to him. In some sad way, I believed this would help bridge the gap between us and wipe away the years of emotional neglect. *At least he cared enough to write me a note*, I could hear him thinking.

From the truck I took a notepad and pen and walked to a nearby hill. (And don't think I didn't try to start the truck one more time, because I did, and, no, it didn't start this time either.) This hill overlooked a picturesque valley. Not a bad place to pen the last thing I would ever write on this earth.

On the small hill, I found a spot and took time to take in the scenery. The soft rays of the January sun warmed me as they broke free from a cluster of white clouds. The birds chirped away high overhead, and the workings of nature began to ease my worried mind. My anxiousness started to fade as I fixed my eyes on the beauty all around. I thought about my friend and counselor Bob Sanders, who'd lost his battle with cancer less than three weeks ago. I missed him.

Still every inch the angry man I was before, I felt my mind-set begin to change, and I thought with a clarity that was unfamiliar to me, especially over these last few dark days.

I thought about God and how I'd come to view Him. I believed Him to be both good and evil and blamed Him for all the terrible things that had happened in my life.

I had the notepad out and began to write:

January 12, 2008

God, I kinda figure You might be here. I kinda think You may exist. I am not quite certain today. I don't love You and am quite certain I DO NOT TRUST YOU. Lord, if You are there or wherever, I could use some help if this is the good side I am talking to.

I believe in the dark side for that's all I have ever known. I believe in Satan because I have seen his works and face.

I've been cut, I have cut myself, I've been killed, and I have killed myself. I have been hurt and I have hurt others.

Lord, if You are real, You need to start talking. You know I am about ready to die. I have this one last note to write to Andrew and that is it.

I can tell You another thing if You are there; Your followers suck! They lie and they are hypocrites. In a moment they quote Scripture and fornicate. They speak Your words, and then they lie to each other. They come to church hours after they lust for their neighbor and commit sin. They say they serve You but are inwardly evil. They profess You, but their eyes and hearts are consumed by this world. God, I could use You right now. Help me.

If You are real, help me now. I've lied and I have killed. I have lied and I have cheated. I have hurt everyone in my life, including You, if You are there.

Oh, God, I have been hurt. You weren't there. I cried every night. You weren't there. I was just a boy, with my little arms, all the freckles, and my stupid little striped shirt. Why? How come, God?

Hey You, Satan took me in, why didn't You? This is it and You know it, God. Help me. Where are You? I need You and not tomorrow.

As I finished writing that prayer, a sudden peace swept over me. A sense of comfort welled up inside of me, in spite of the spiritual battle that was raging, relief amid this violent storm. Then the squirrels, rabbits, and birds seemed to vanish. The cool breeze slowed to a stop, and the sky started to fade. The path I walked in on melted into the surrounding fields. Then I saw something coming I'd never seen before.

To my left were dark, shadowy figures, and to my right and straight ahead were large, white images. A battle seemed to ensue between the white figures and the dark figures, and the air around me whirled with turbulence. During this spiritual dustup, one moment I felt a great heaviness, and the next moment I felt peace and security. My body seemed to melt into the landscape. I was conscious and alert but unaware of my physical body.

In a voice that seemed like a whisper, I heard, *"Stop it, stop it, stop it, stop it . . . stop it. What is your petition?"*

Without speaking I asked, *God?*

I then heard, *"I created you!"*

A feeling of complete peace washed over me. I grabbed my pen and paper and began to write. Awestruck over the words that were spoken to me, I felt warm, safe, and protected. In an instant, I felt whole again. That something had taken my brokenness and returned it to its proper form. My pulse quickened. I breathed faster, like an excited child who has just discovered a marvelous surprise and is too excited for words.

I heard the voice in my spirit say to me:

Michael, I chose that name. I chose you first. Take up your cross. Ask anything. Your only strength is in Me. Surrender totally. Submit your spirit to Mine. I will give you eyes. You shall see again. My sheep hear My voice. Your shelter is in Me. Carry the message; pray for Chris. Trust. You were tight with angels before. Speak the Word. Bob Sanders is safe, warm, and secure. Be not afraid, Michael. Let you have peace now. Let you understand now. Let others see Me through you. Pray for the nation. Pray for the afflicted. Your gifts are from Me. Satan is defeated. Receive all I have for you. Your thoughts are being cleansed. Your time is near. Fight. I will silence your foes. Let your light so shine. Fight. I will comfort your heart. I will make you a leader of men. I will. I have. I am. Fight. My Word shall possess you. Teach others. Holy, holy, holy. Renounce Satan and his works. Forgive all. You are a warrior, Michael. I will quiet your mind and give you peace. I will never leave you. You will never leave Me again. You are in My hands; you are in My arms. I have sent My angels to protect you and your house. I have placed many around you so that you may trust.

I felt as if the Word of God was being absorbed in the cells of my body. All I could say was, "I need You. I want You. Lord, I want You in my life. I am so, so sorry, Lord."

What seemed like hours passed before I tried to move. Slowly I felt my body return to me again. I regained my senses as if I were returning from a deep, deep sleep. I didn't have the strength to stand. I felt the presence of something very large behind me help me to my feet. I heard the sound of distant laughter and men's voices.

Trying to process what just happened to me, I walked slowly back to my truck. I got in, turned the key, and finally heard the truck start. I stared through the windshield, trying to make sense of it all, when I noticed the guys returning from their games.

Voices from the back of the cabin drew me out of the truck and to a group of men sitting and talking. I was still a little dazed and slightly incoherent, but the four men began speaking to me. We carried on with small talk for a few minutes. From their expressions, I knew they were seeing a different man. Someone much different from the man they'd known the night before. That moment gave me hope, but did I have some explaining to do!

To Frank Stotts, one of the men sitting nearby, I said, "I have a story. Does anyone care to hear it?"

Ernie Flowers and Brett Andersen looked at me with caution, likely remembering how distant, rude, and angry I had been since arriving at the complex. Another member smiled and gave me an encouraging look.

A long pause ensued before Brett smiled and said, "Praise God, let's rock and roll."

Ernie prayed, and we headed to a quiet place in the cabin.

I really don't recall much about what was said over the next hour. From what I heard, the process of deliverance occurred—the men casting out demons until I could say Jesus is Lord of my life. Brett Andersen led me to a place of receiving Christ! I understand now that on the hill, I submitted my spirit to the Lord.

The men cut loose, praising God. The Lord told me that we needed to read Psalm 119. We all were praising God while one of the men read the scripture out loud.

Immediately after my profession in the cabin, the Lord let me know I needed to be baptized. So the men filled a bathtub, and I climbed in. Frank Stotts, with his hands gently trembling, asked me, "Michael, I just witnessed that you received Christ in your life. Brett asked you a series of questions and explained to you the Word of God regarding salvation. For those of us who witnessed this, it is our belief, based on the holy Word of God, that you are born again and are a new creature, a new creation. Is it your will to be baptized as an expression of your desire to have a new life in Jesus Christ?"

With tears of joy brimming in my eyes, I said, "Yes!"

As my now brothers in Christ crowded into that small bathroom, Frank lowered me under the water, and then I heard him say, "Michael, I now baptize you in the name of the Father, the Son, and the Holy Spirit!"

As Frank lowered me, my mind flashed back to a time at the beach when I was a young boy and a woman held me underwater, trying to choke the breath out of me. I saw the hands of the woman trying to harm me. I saw the sunlight pouring into the water. I saw it so clearly, that boy . . . that woman . . .

But when Frank raised me from the water in the tub, I saw the face of Jesus. He spoke into my spirit: *"I saved you then, and I'm saving you now."* Peace like I'd never known flowed through my body and spirit. I was renewed. Now I knew real power, the power to change a wicked heart, and I couldn't get close enough to it.

While I was still praising God, the Lord told me that He wanted us to turn to Acts 2 and read aloud. As the Holy Spirit filled that room and every man in it, the next hour or so was incredible. We've all been to parties, but probably not one like this: this was the best one I ever attended.

That night, I made a personal request: that God would never allow me to be lukewarm in my faith, that He'd take my life before He'd allow that to happen.

God's response made me chuckle: *"Son, you have never been lukewarm."*

That night I fell into a deep, restful sleep—the first time I had ever slept peacefully. The next morning, when everyone woke up, we ate and had time to share what had happened the night before. The men discussed the retreat, what it had meant to each, and then we dismissed with prayer.

As I drove down Highway 33 east toward I-35, the Holy Spirit reminded me that my mother had spent the last few years at a nursing home on this very road. I was estranged from my mother and had only seen her a couple of times in the last six years, but something compelled me to stop. Maggie and I had taken the kids in to see her about six months ago, but that was the last time we'd spoken.

I pulled into the parking lot, wondering what I would say to my mother. I went to the nurses' station and signed in. The receptionist informed me that my mother still didn't recognize anyone. The nurse directed me to her room. She told me a family friend had last been in about a year ago, and besides my visit six months ago, that was her only visitor. It stung to hear the nurse say this. No relatives, no visitors, no friends.

I eased my way into my mom's room and stood in the doorway. She turned to me, her face a blank stare. She looked clean and well cared for, and her eyes were bright as she said hello as if greeting a stranger.

I moved closer and knelt down next to her bed. I took her hand in mine. It was downy soft, and I squeezed it tenderly as a flood of memories came rushing back. Tears flowed down my cheeks as I looked around the room. No personal belongings, no pictures, no reminders of family, friends, or better times were displayed.

Her memories had been stolen. Nothing but a bed, a nightstand, a lamp, a chair, and hard, cold, tile floors surrounded her.

I looked at my mother's face and with a quivering voice said, "Hi, Mom." She leaned forward on the edge of her bed. I continued, "Mom, I was just at a men's church retreat." Her smile told me she didn't understand what I told her. I bowed my head and was staring at the floor as I said, "I just wanted to tell you that I gave my heart to Jesus! I can't describe all that happened, but I can tell you the Lord spoke to me, and I am His now. I want to live for God. I believe His Son died on the cross for me and for you!"

I looked up and not only saw a soft smile, but I saw tears flowing from her eyes. "And Mom, I just wanted to say I am sorry I wasn't the best son. I am sorry you were hurt when you were young. I am sorry I haven't stayed in touch. Mom, I forgive you. I hope you can forgive me."

I stared into her tear-filled eyes. "Mom . . ." My voice broke. I hugged her as I tried to regain my composure. I wiped my face with the back of my hand, then continued. "Mom, God sent His Son, Jesus, for you too. Jesus died on the cross for your sins and my sins and for the sins of the world. All we have to do is allow Him into our hearts and accept Him as Lord and Savior!"

She seemed to be understanding me, so I asked, "Mom, do you care if I pray?"

For the first time, she seemed to be speaking directly to me: "Of course not, son."

My prayer went something like this: "Lord, thank You so much for Your mercy and grace. Thank You, God, for my salvation; thank You for the retreat. God, help me to know You more deeply. Lord, I ask You to help my mom, I ask You to let her realize Your mercy and power like You have shown me. Jesus, show

Yourself to my mother if You haven't already. God, I don't know what else to say . . . I've never been this formal with You. I hope that was okay, God." I'd smiled at the frankness of my last comment as I pulled back and looked again into my mother's tender face. Tears pooled in her eyes. Maybe, just maybe, she understood every single word.

"I love you, Mom."

Although my mother could hardly speak, I believe her heart shone through her tearful eyes and God was at work in her life. That is my hope, my belief. I didn't know at the time that my mother would die only a few weeks later. I'm so thankful that God, in His grace, prompted me to go see her one last time and pray for her.

✝

On Sunday, January 13—the day the enemy had determined for my death—I was more alive than I had ever been. Filled with the joy of my new life in Christ, I sat in the front row in LifeChurch's 11:30 a.m. service to worship and praise the God who saved me.

As the music began, I received a text from head of security John Zeigler asking which service I would attend. I responded quickly with *"This one,"* and he asked where I was. He had scanned the crowd and didn't see me in my assigned seat. A security breach was in progress.

I texted back telling him to look to the left of where he was sitting. I was in the front row, center stage. I can't imagine what went through the minds of the pastors and security guards when they saw me—the man who had been instructed to kill their pastor—on the front row, hands in the air, praising God, joyful and free. If they were suspicious at first, I couldn't blame them. But soon they all knew something unmistakable had happened: I'd become a walking miracle, and they could see it. Many tears were shed by pastors and faithful saints whose intercessory prayers had been faithfully answered.

To this day, I sit in the same seat when I attend church: the same place the Lord told me to sit when I attended for the first time after my salvation. I will always sit in the front of the church to glorify God in the way I need to. Because, being the wretched sinner I was, I have so much to be grateful for.

Maybe you do too. That's how we're alike, you and I: we're just sinners who need Jesus. Remember, no matter how badly you think you've sinned or what kind of mess you may have made of your life, it probably pales in comparison to mine. Never give up, never lose hope. Jesus Christ specializes in fixing broken messes just like us. He is, and always will be, the great Redeemer, and He is ready to transform your life whenever you call out to Him. Why can I tell you this? Just look what He did for me.

I had a life-changing and dramatic experience with the Creator of the universe. He showed me His mercy and grace, forgave my sin, and saved me out of a life of evil, darkness, and pain.

Today, I no longer ask the question, "Why am I here?" but rather, "God, what would You have me do?"

EPILOGUE

THE ROAD HOME

But whatever were gains to me I now consider loss for the sake of Christ. What is more, I consider everything a loss because of the surpassing worth of knowing Christ Jesus my Lord, for whose sake I have lost all things. I consider them garbage, that I may gain Christ and be found in him, not having a righteousness of my own that comes from the law, but that which is through faith in Christ— the righteousness that comes from God on the basis of faith.

—PHILIPPIANS 3:7–9

After the church service, I went home and immediately put a worship CD in my stereo. Someone used to leave "Christian presents" at my door. This particular CD had appeared three months earlier, gift wrapped with some homemade trail mix and a candle. I knew it was in the house somewhere, so I found it and chose "Shout to the Lord," by Darlene Zschech. I pressed the Repeat button. That song would play over and over, twenty-four hours a day, in my house for the next four months. I believe my dog could even sing the words to the tune. It was a song I could identify with. All I wanted to do was shout to the Lord and praise Him! The very thing I despised

219

before, I now loved. I loved standing in my living room, closing my eyes, lifting my hands in praise, and singing to the Lord!

Another song I love to praise and worship God with is an old one. Remember my saying in an earlier chapter I was haunted by a song I heard while visiting a church function? Yep, "You Are My All in All," by Dennis Jernigan. I love that song. And I have come to know the songwriter as well. We are now friends and meet occasionally for fellowship and encouragement. I have never said this before but will now: *Take that, Satan!*

I walked up the stairs at a brisk pace, on a mission. I went to my bedroom and slung open the sliding door. I stepped outside and went directly to the rope that hung over the edge of the upstairs deck, awaiting my planned suicide. I pulled out my pocketknife. The knife that once was used to inflict injury and pain was now going to be used to cut down the rope that represented Satan's power over me.

As I cut the rope, watching it drop ten feet to the ground, I said, "Satan, never again will you rule me. From now on, anytime I feel you are coming against me or those I love, I will witness Jesus to at least five people that very day. Begone! Out of my life! I denounce you and your works! I repent to my Lord for having ever served you and your wicked ways. Father God, forgive and protect me, my family, and your followers in my life!" I watched the rope fall to the ground, and with it, the whole burden of my past.

I felt a surge within me as I got off one knee and stood up. I felt like never before, clean and fresh of spirit, rested and revitalized of mind. It was as if I were a young child again, innocent and pure. I knew to give God the glory for what He had done in me. I knew He was with me. I felt as though He smiled as He held me close. I felt completely loved for the first time in my life.

✝

In the days and weeks after my salvation, my life truly changed. I could see more clearly; colors seemed to stand out vividly. I could smell more intensely. Food tasted better. Each day that passed seemed to be brighter, and for once in my life, I had a real smile on my face. I experienced little depression or sadness. I was not consumed with the thought of dying. I wanted to live.

The heaviness I once felt was gone. Anxiety and worry faded with each passing day. Fears I had once experienced were gone. The peace of the Lord was on me, and I wasn't about to let it go. I had a new mission: to share what had happened to me with the world.

LifeChurch.tv continued to be my church home when I was in Edmond. My church family is awesome. The love they showed me in my darkest days—and the way they continue to love me and mentor me—is unbelievable. I began attending several LifeChurch services to interact with the thousands of members who gathered weekly. I also visited other local churches to hear the messages being taught and to study the preaching style of the many pastors. I would soon have the opportunity to speak in front of many and share my testimony. I was confident that God had a calling for my life, and part of that calling meant sharing my testimony and His Word and ministering to congregations of all sizes.

I attended at least three life groups per week. I was asked to speak at local men's groups and teenage events. God showed me in the book of Acts that as soon as Ananias laid his hands on the apostle Paul and the scales fell off his eyes, Paul began to preach in the synagogues (Acts 9:20). The Lord told me always to hear His voice and to know I would have many come against me, both inside and outside His church. The hardest attacks would be from those I love and from those inside the church body. God instructed me to focus only on Him, that the storms of life would not go away, but He would be there continually to see me through and guide me!

As I look back over my life, I'm astounded at God's relentless pursuit of me. Even when I was far away from Him, He arranged circumstances and sent people into my life to guide my stumbling steps toward His light. And now that I am focused on serving Him, God has continued to direct my path from event to event.

Through my good friend Darius McGlory, I was introduced to Joe Thomas, who became a mentor and teacher to me. Joe is eighty-seven years old at the time of writing and is an ordained pastor. He has been in the Word for more than seventy years and is a bold and outspoken Christ follower. We continue to spend many days a week together, learning Scripture and witnessing to others. Both of us have ministries that intertwine as we progress toward the goal of speaking God's truth and seeing others set free from bondage, addiction, and misinformation.

Today, Pastor Joe and I sit on the front row of our church and during praise and worship occasionally dance to the tunes through the prompting of the Holy Spirit. We enjoy our time together each week, and it is an honor for me to have him in my life. We have much in common, including a no-nonsense approach in taking God's Word to the streets everywhere we go.

In Edmond, David Barnes and I hang together at a coffee shop called All about Cha nearly every day. I may be writing in my journal, starting a new book, or just studying the Word while David is on his computer, conducting business or just talking about what the Lord is doing in his life. In fact, about twenty of my fellow LifeChurchers gather daily at this coffee shop. It is a haven for great cuisine, the best coffee, and tremendous fellowship.

But our journeys don't end after we accept Jesus Christ as Lord and Savior. We still have a continuing purpose He wants us to fulfill in sharing this new life with others.

It has been incredible and faith-building to witness what the Lord does every day in my life. The Lord is glorified through many awe-inspiring happenings. In the eleven months I have hung out at the coffee shop, more than a thousand people have come in and spoken to me about faith, God, Christ, and the Bible. I always have a Bible open, not only for reference and study, but for a witness as well. The Bible seems to draw people to sit near me. Either they share their interests in the Word and the Lord or their opinions on how they do not believe in God.

✝

In the three years since my salvation, my life has changed dramatically. The clarity of thought God gives me is amazing. Each day I talk to anyone who will listen to my story. Wherever I go, I am open to speak about God's grace and love. The Scripture flows from my mouth. I feel an intense urge to edify and encourage others. I have never looked back; I am only concerned with what each day will bring.

I am doing my best to be led by the Spirit of the Lord. At times, I fail and sin. I get distracted and have to strive to be *in* this world and not *of* it. Satan is the tempter, so I have to submit to the Lord, repent, and keep moving forward in obedience. I have to choose continually to serve God and be obedient to His commandments, but more than that, to be in relationship with Him. I have to choose this day and every day whom and what I am serving.

I fight depression. I fight finances. I fight my flesh. I get tired of the battles. I am not good enough and cannot work hard enough to gain either man's or God's approval of me. But I do not need to. I need only to submit and relinquish control of myself continually to my God, and He will do the rest. Over and over, God loves me out of my sin and into His gracious arms. Instead of avoiding God during times of temptation and failure, I actually pray for sanctification and correction!

It has always been a big step for me to relinquish control. But the benefit of letting go and giving all my cares and worries to Him has been well worth the act of faith. He gives me freedom and peace that continue to grow my faith. My submission to God enables Him to act in my life to fulfill the promises of His Word. The more victory I have in Him, the easier it gets to pour more of myself into Him. The more I see how faithful He is to me, the easier it is to trust in Him and just let go of anything that comes between Him and me.

I have learned the only thing that evil can take over is darkness. Darkness invades our lives when we shut out the light of God's love. But where there is light, there cannot be darkness. Light pierces darkness and illuminates the truth.

We must realize that we are in a world that is spiritually intertwined. There is more to our existence than the obvious. *We must open our eyes* to see the spiritual realm, which is very real and very powerful. And we must learn the weapons of our adversary, not only to avoid becoming ensnared by darkness but to be able to reach into that darkness to rescue others, like me, with the light. We are instruments of change. We are powerful vessels carrying an eternal cargo of either life or death.

The reason for sharing my story in this book is to demonstrate the power of God over Satan and to show how merciful a God we have in heaven. To give Him the glory and praise, to demonstrate the power of love over fear, to show the love our Father has for us, to let God's light expose the darkness—but mainly to facilitate the hope that by reading this story, people might turn to the King of kings!

I pray that my story gives you hope that no matter how far away you are from the Lord, He is near. He knocks on the door and simply and politely asks if you will let Him in. His only reason for wanting in is to give you peace and direction in your life. He loves His creation. He loves you. He has a will for your life, the perfect life for you that will bring perfect happiness and direction for you.

The Scripture tells us that it isn't the Lord's will that anyone should perish, but that all should come to have everlasting life (John 3:16; 2 Peter 3:9).

God doesn't promise a smooth road or a path that is free of troubles, problems, and rough times. He does promise that no matter what you are going through, He will be there with you. He will comfort you. He will give you strength. He will give you a peace that cannot be put into human words. He will give you eternal salvation in His perfect presence.

Through all the experiences and trials of my life and through my salvation, I have come to a scripture that is my favorite, Job

19:25: "I know that my redeemer lives, and that in the end he will stand on the earth." With all I have seen in the spirit and all I have been freed from, I know my Redeemer lives.

I pray that, like me, you will turn to Christ and find that place of hope, freedom, and peace.

SURROUNDED BY A GREAT CLOUD OF WITNESSES

Therefore, since we are surrounded by such a great cloud
of witnesses, let us throw off everything that hinders
and the sin that so easily entangles. And let us run with
perseverance the race marked out for us, fixing our eyes
on Jesus, the pioneer and perfecter of faith. For the joy
set before him he endured the cross, scorning its shame,
and sat down at the right hand of the throne of God.
Consider him who endured such opposition from sinners,
so that you will not grow weary and lose heart.

—HEBREWS 12:1–3

I'm so thankful for the men and women God placed in my life to encourage me and guide me toward the gospel, especially during my darkest days. These are a few of the testimonies from men and women who know me well and attest that everything in this book is true—and that our God can do anything!

David Barnes

As marketing director for a consulting firm, I worked with great people, got to travel a little, and used our office conference room as a meeting place for my men's accountability group. The guys in my men's group were like family. They had walked me through job issues, marriage issues, and children issues and were all good friends.

Doug Warren was part of that group. For several meetings, he came with a prayer request for one of his neighbors. He would walk through the neighborhood and observe this very intense man working in his yard at all hours of the day and night. Doug felt led to pray for him and then invited him to our men's group. That's how I was introduced to Michael Leehan.

Mike showed up at that first meeting looking like a very disturbed man. I sensed a man who was very unhappy with a lot on his mind. After going through our normal routine, we came to that part of the meeting where we discussed issues we needed to pray about. I asked Mike if he was a believer, and he said he wasn't sure. I asked him if we could pray for him, and he said, "Okay . . . as long as you don't touch me."

Nothing had prepared me for the journey I was about to take with Mike Leehan. We began to pray. I don't think, to this day, I can adequately describe the events that took place in our meeting that night. Three hours after we started, I found myself facedown on the floor, asking God to do His work because I knew it was a situation I was completely helpless to control. There was a presence of evil in that room that I had never experienced before. We all fought back through prayer. It was clear that it was Mike this presence was emanating through, yet there was a compassion I was given for this man that left me with the knowledge that God's hand was all over this.

The meeting ended around 1 a.m. The next day, I got calls from every guy who was there asking me, "What happened?"

Mike was invited back to the next meeting. I had already decided to bring one of our pastors, Robert Wall, to meet this guy.

I don't remember much about the next meeting. Robert sat at one end of the conference table and Mike at the other. There were very few words spoken. It was more of a staredown. It was like there was a battle going on spiritually that none of us could see, but there were no words spoken. It was very bizarre.

Bizarre is also the word I would use to describe what happened next. Mike, after just a couple of meetings and a few conversations, looked at me and said, "I think you're supposed to go to work for me." I let him know I was very happy with my job and wasn't looking to make a move. The next day at work, the owner of the company took me out for a three-hour lunch to break the news that he was eliminating my position. I called Mike and asked him what he had in mind. Looking back, I can't imagine what I was thinking in going to work for a guy I had just gone through these experiences with. A few weeks later, I found myself an employee of Doorways USA, doing a job I had never dreamed I would ever do. I met Mike's business partner, who, after warning me about what I was getting into, gave me a large sack full of books on deliverance, freedom ministry, and the occult. It was one of those "What did I get myself into?" moments.

As it turned out, I was very good at the position he put me in and very much enjoyed my relationship with Mike and the direction he was taking the company in. Under most circumstances, this was a dream job. Things were very normal at work, and Mike ran a very lucrative business. He had an obvious skill level in building relationships with his customers and running a very efficient company. Below the surface, there was some stuff going on.

As I got to know Mike better, I was very careful with the situations and circumstances I found myself dealing with. The greatest result of this was in my prayer life. I knew I couldn't handle what I was involved in without the power of God on my side. I prayed . . . a lot. There was a side of Mike I knew I needed to be careful with, but as our relationship grew, he was very careful to treat me as an employee he respected and even as a friend. My first challenge was when Mike asked me to go on a trip through Kansas, New Mexico, and Texas to take care of some work he had lined up. We hopped in his truck and headed out the door. The trip was uneventful until we stopped at a Kicks 66 station for fuel.

One of the first things you notice about Mike's appearance is the scars on his arms. Part of the rituals he took part in involved cutting his arms and inviting demons in through his blood. His arms are covered with these scars. As we approached the register to pay for our fuel, the young man behind the counter took a long look at Mike's arms. I immediately noticed he had the same scars on his arms. Not as many, but they were there. Mike had a handful of change, and the attendant noticed a coin mixed in with some writing on it. Mike picked it up, turned it over to reveal the cross on it, and explained that "it was a God thing" and that his daughter had given it to him. The young man mumbled something I didn't understand and then something that I did understand. He said, "You're going to die soon." People around us were staring. Mike laughed and said, "Probably so." As we were walking out the door, I asked Mike to clarify what this guy said. He explained that the guy was a satanist and they put a death curse on anyone who tried to leave this lifestyle. As we were getting in the truck, the speaker mounted over the gas tanks crackled and a very strange voice said, "You heard me." Chills. We got in the truck and headed down the road.

I had invited Mike to my house a number of times for our small group Bible study. The few times he came, the result was always the same: Mike would show up, sit for a few minutes, and start wheezing. He would have such a hard time breathing he would have to get up and leave. As soon as we left the gas station, the wheezing started again. Mike's eyes glazed over. This was a real problem to me because he was driving. The situation got more intense when Mike pulled out a black knife, one I found out later he used in various rituals. He placed the blade against his arm and started putting pressure on to cut himself. I'm not sure why, but I didn't panic. I reached over and took the knife out of his hands. I called a friend with extensive experience dealing with this and, between her council and a lot of prayer, made it through the situation and home safely without anything else happening.

The next six months, I spent a tremendous amount of time on the road. When I was back at the office, Mike and I spent a lot of time together. Our friendship grew, and I used every occasion I could to bring up God and the happiness a relationship with Christ would bring. During this part of our relationship, I felt very protected and confident in my relationship with Christ. This never changed, but the circumstances and my relationship with Mike did.

Mike called me into his office one day and asked if I would be interested in managing his contractors nationwide. This was the position he had originally hired me for, but I really enjoyed what I was doing on the road. Though the change would require me to be in the office most of the time, I decided to accept.

Working with Mike on an everyday basis was quite the adventure. There were days that I had more fun than I've ever had anywhere. This was a time Mike refers to as his "double-minded" days. I knew he wanted to make a decision to serve Christ, but he was so addicted to the power he felt from the dark side that it was hard for him to let go. The bad days could be very bizarre. He would find weaknesses in people and exploit them in every way. Sometimes it was to get something he wanted, and sometimes it appeared to be just for fun.

As the months dragged on, Mike became more distant. One of our major customers bought out some of our other customers, and it put the company in a dangerous position. We ended up losing this account, and this added to the confusion and chaos that seemed to be growing within the company.

On the ministry side, I often solicited help from friends who had experiences and knowledge I felt might be helpful to me. One of these individuals was Larry Ladd. Larry had walked through some extraordinary life experiences and often used these experiences to help minister to others. I arranged for Larry and Mike to meet for breakfast one morning. We had what I thought was a typical conversation. We spent about an hour just talking about Mike's belief system and some of the things he struggled with. He seemed to feel comfortable with Larry and opened up with him. As we were leaving, I let Mike drive off, and Larry and I stayed and visited for a few minutes. My first question was, "What do you think?" Larry said, "I felt like I just had a conversation with about seven different people."

A few weeks later, I got a call from Mike at 2 a.m. It was clear the internal struggle was getting to him. I asked if he would like to meet me at the prayer chapel on the Edmond LifeChurch campus, and he agreed. I got in touch with Larry, and he met us there. Larry and I started praying. For whatever reason, Mike wouldn't speak. I can't tell you if he was unable to or just wouldn't, but he seemed very upset. He would write notes to us, as if he was afraid someone would hear him if he spoke. He wrote a scripture on one of the pieces of paper and handed it to me. I believe it was Hebrews 10:19–25.

I asked Mike what the scripture was, and he wouldn't answer. I opened my Bible and started to look it up, and Larry, as he looked at the piece of paper, said, "I know what it is." Larry said that before he left he called his brother and told him where he was going. His brother gave him that same scripture and told him we needed to "plead the blood of Jesus over him." As we prayed, a peace seemed to fall over the room. The tense look Mike carried on his face most of the time seemed to relax, and he actually became so relaxed he fell asleep. Larry and I just quietly talked as he slept. It was a peaceful moment.

Spiritually, Mike continued to go back and forth. At work, the condition of the company worsened. Mike seemed to stay in an agitated frame of mind. I was a convenient person for him to vent his frustration to. He would blame me for struggles the company was having, but never directly. The blame would come through e-mails to his CFO. He would have discussions regarding the condition of the company and what my role was in resolving them . . . or not getting them resolved. The e-mails would appear to be confidential, but he would always copy me on them. He was angry with me all the time, and very suspicious.

One Friday morning, I was working at my desk. It was a typical workday. Out of nowhere, Mike came rushing through the door into my office. As he was walking in, he looked over his shoulder and said, "You got my back, Satan." He proceeded to curse at me and tell me how deceitful and untrustworthy I was. He told me to get out of the office. He fired me and said he never wanted to see me in the office again. He continued to curse at me as I gathered some personal belongings and left. I felt a great sense of peace through the entire ordeal. I went home and prayed both for Mike and for wherever this new journey would take me.

I got a call from Mike at home that night. He apologized and let me know what a valuable friend I was. He said he would like me to consider coming back to work. I told him I would pray about it over the weekend. I went to the office Monday morning and walked in on a sales meeting Mike was conducting. It was rare to see Mike get emotional back then. He was apologizing to the staff and letting them know he had called me and apologized and asked me to come back. He told them I was a valued friend and employee and he had made an error in letting me go. It was the closest I had ever seen him to shedding tears.

The next few weeks were back and forth. There were good days and bad days. I had a continuing uneasiness about being there as the oppressive atmosphere at the office continued to grow. Through my prayers, I felt God telling me that my time there was almost over. Mike needed to get to a point where he made the decision to be a Christ follower on his own. I couldn't talk him into it. I went home one Friday evening and told my wife I didn't think I could go back. I didn't have another job lined up, and my financial condition was not the best. I certainly didn't have enough money to carry my family for very long. I called one of the guys in my accountability group and explained the situation and how I was feeling. He agreed that my season there needed to end. He told me, "God is always faithful. It's easy to trust Him with the little things, but when you trust Him with the big things, it's an opportunity for Him to show His faithfulness." I sat down and wrote my resignation letter.

My wife and I had a number of discussions about our situation over the weekend. We were not angry with Mike. In fact, our compassion for him was the greatest it had ever been. She told me we needed to continue to pray for him and that she knew God had a great ministry ahead for him, despite what the circumstances were now. She also said we were not to speak anything but blessings over Mike. I agreed. I went to work with my letter in hand, completely peaceful about my decision.

Mike was not in Monday morning. I will never forget my walk down the hallway to the office of Alfredo, our CFO. Alfredo was a very nice guy but intensely loyal to Mike and the company. I had one brief interruption. My cell phone, a company phone, rang one last time. I answered a call from Doug Reeves. Doug was a friend from church I hadn't spoken to in a number of months. He called to get my address so he could send me his daughter's graduation announcement. He asked what I was doing, and I told him. It was good to talk to a friend at that moment. Doug told me to come by and see him after I left the office. I turned in my letter of resignation to Alfredo. I was immediately asked to leave the building. The next few days, I received a barrage of e-mails from Mike letting me know what a lousy employee I was. I could sense a lot of hurt and anger, but I ignored the e-mails and ceased contact with Mike.

I went by Doug's home office. Doug owned a small business selling to the electric utility industry. Within a week Doug had offered me a position with his company, and I accepted.

Other than one brief sighting of Mike at a home improvement

store, I didn't see or talk to him for a little over a year. My season with Doug was a blessing, but I made a career change that would eventually allow me to bless other ministries. I was sitting in a local restaurant with the owners of the company I worked with. Out of nowhere, a french fry hit me in the side of the face. I looked over and saw Michael Leehan laughing. Mike told me he had accepted Christ and his life had changed drastically. I saw a difference in him during our brief meeting, but was still skeptical. I agreed to call him for coffee the following week. It took about three weeks for me to actually pick up the phone. Mike and I got together, and he told me the incredible story of his conversion. Mike and I spent a lot of time together over the next few months. I've never seen anyone exhibit such a dramatic change in personality. His business was gone, his girlfriend was gone, and he was doing contract work as a carpenter. He was making a fraction of the money he made when I worked for him, yet I had never seen anyone as joyful or as peaceful. He told me he would rather go without earthly possessions if it meant losing what he had. He called it "the sweet breath of Jesus two inches from his face breathing life into him every day."

It's been almost two and a half years since that french fry hit me in the face. I spend more time with Mike than anyone other than my family. I've watched him minister to countless people, including very close friends of mine. I've watched as he quickly takes correction from the Holy Spirit and stands defiant when something he knows is from God goes against the grain of "religious" acquaintances. I continue to see bizarre things happen around him. As he wrote this book, we spent a tremendous amount of time in a local coffee house. Several friends were sitting around listening as Mike was involved in a discussion with a gentleman interested in seeing Mike's work published or put into a movie. A number of us noticed a pale man sitting in a corner close to the door. He was reading a book but kept looking up and staring in our direction. No one said anything until he suddenly held the book up for us to see what he was reading. It was the *Book of Shadows*. He disappeared shortly after that. One of the restaurant managers Mike had become friends with came over and asked if we knew the strange man who had been sitting in the corner. Situations like this still happen, but Mike handles them with the confidence I know comes through the Holy Spirit.

Today, I support Mike and his ministry. Mike and I have been through junk that would permanently destroy most relationships. Forgiveness that could only come through a sincere relationship with Christ and the power of the Holy Spirit has turned it into a relationship that is full of laughter and great expectation for the cause of Christ. It is a testament to the power of Jesus, because, after all that has taken place, Mike is my friend.

Joe Thomas

I want to thank Darius McGlory for suggesting to Mike that he get to know me. I have known Mike the past two years and have spent hours in Bible study and in sharing my testimony with him. I showed how Jesus had delivered me from the spirit of lust that had embarrassed me many times as a Baptist pastor. Jesus also broke the generational curses of lust, divorce, disease, poverty, debt, and early death that badly plagued my family.

Since I knew more about Satan and evil spirits than the average Joe, Mike and I shared some common ground. However, he taught me a lot about satanism that I did not know. I shared with Mike from my seventy years of Bible study and my experiences in deliverance ministry. I have faced spirits of homosexuality, cruelty, lust, witchcraft, murder, gluttony, and fear, to name a few. The name of Jesus prevailed and the spirits left, defeated.

Mike and I often met at Denny's or Starbucks and interacted with the waitstaff and customers. One waitress broke down and wept as Mike "read her mail." We were able to pray for her and share the comfort of the Lord with her. She was very touched with our caring about her and sharing God's love.

Mike's word of knowledge excited me as I saw this spiritual gift in action. For example, we were in church during praise and worship one evening. A few rows behind us sat a young man perhaps in his early twenties. No one sat between the young man and Mike. Mike said, "The Lord tells me you have an alcohol problem. You promised you would stop. In fact, the Lord tells me you were indulging last night. You need to make a choice. Either serve the Lord or the drink."

Tears poured down the young man's cheeks. Then he told us later that he was drunk the night before and felt very guilty. He met us after service at Denny's, where we talked and prayed with him. He bought our meal and said he felt we loved him and could feel the love of Jesus speak to him. I ran into him a few months ago, and he reported that he has not had a drink since.

I sit with Mike on the front row of church every Sunday we attend. After his testimony was shared with the church, many people recognize Mike and come forth for prayer and ministry each week. One night, a teenage "cutter" came with her mother. She gave her heart to the Lord and her razor blades to her mother that evening as Mike ministered to them. Her mother asked that

I serve them Communion, which I did, as I read Scripture and prayed for them.

Mike as a new convert had some rough edges and one severe test after another. Once, at a gas station, a man reared up in Mike's face and spat upon him. This man cursed at Mike and mistreated him badly. Mike warned the man to get away from him or he would break his nose. The man continued to taunt Mike. So Mike broke his nose. The police and medics came. No charges were filed against Mike, as many witnesses reported the man's actions and Mike's initial patience. Later, I read Mike some scriptures, including 2 Corinthians 10:4—"The weapons we fight with are not the weapons of the world"—and told him that he should have prayed for the man instead of hurting him. Mike listened and said he did pray for the man: he prayed for healing after the altercation! I guess in reality, if there ever came a time when I was physically threatened, I would want Mike there.

Mike is a no-frills type of guy. He carries himself well, but I don't imagine too many men, either bigger or younger, would want to tangle with him. He walks with a kind of authority that demands respect. His eyes tell of his past and without much imagination would hold at bay most would-be confrontations. I can certainly see why many are glad he came to the Lord!

I do enjoy being with Mike with his prophetic giftings and his boldness in Christ. As I fellowshipped and prayed with him, our bond brought new blessings to me.

Mike told me something I never have thought of. He said, "Satan thinks he is going to win, Pastor Joe. He has deceived himself. He is the father of lies and doesn't know the truth!" That may seem a simple statement to most, but it is very profound to me and something I never thought of.

Satan will never give up until he is sealed in the place prepared for him. How will he fare when he faces all those he deceived, manipulated, lied to, and killed before they could meet God? By the grace of God, I plan to be a long place from hell!

Mike has endured severe tests, mostly from religious people, but also directly from Satan himself. I have seen Mike get tested on every front and every area of his life and have seen major growth in Christ, endurance I have never witnessed before, and unshakable determination to spread the Word of God. Romans 8:18 says, "I consider that our present sufferings are not worth comparing with the glory that will be revealed in us." This verse is applicable in Mike's life and is one he stands on. This should be one we all stand on!

Mike Leehan could very well be one of the most dangerous opponents to the kingdom of darkness alive today.

Gregg Gun

A couple of years ago, my brother Nathan was part of a men's group. Mike Leehan was in that group too, and my brother told me an incredible account of how Mike had come to Christ during a men's retreat some months earlier. It was such an amazing story, so compelling, so fantastic, so gripping, that I felt a tremendous sense of urgency to meet Mike myself. I wanted to understand firsthand exactly what thoughts and events could have drawn him out of the horror of the dark side into a life in the light.

When Mike and I met, I immediately felt a kindred spirit with him. We just clicked. Both of us consider ourselves to be on a constant journey to see God work in our lives in a more powerful way each day. In John 17:11, Jesus prayed, "Holy Father, protect [my disciples] by the power of your name, the name you gave me, so that they may be one as we are one." That's exactly the kind of oneness I felt with Mike.

Even though Mike was at the time a brand-new believer, I could already see fruit all over his life. As we continued meeting together and talking over the next several months, Mike shared his entire testimony with me. Realizing that his story had the potential for tremendous impact, I wanted as many other people to hear it as possible. I asked Mike to come lead a youth Bible study in our home for some high school and college-aged kids who were friends with my kids. When word got around that Mike was coming, and about what he would be talking about, around twenty-five kids showed up. As we sat in my living room, Mike shared not only what God had done to set him free from his past, but also the things God was continuing to do in his life. The power that Mike is able to tap into in the spirit world is awesome, and the Lord used him in a mighty way. That night, several kids surrendered their hearts and lives totally to Christ.

A few weeks later, we offered another Bible study at my office, where there was more room. Forty to fifty people showed up. One group that came consisted of several skeptical young people who attended seminary at a local Christian university. At the beginning, they politely listened to Mike as he shared his personal testimony of radical life change. However, once Mike opened up to questions, it became evident that the only reason they had come was to grill him on the finer points of his biblical doctrine. They obviously had a game plan worked out in advance. Their questions were designed not to receive understanding, but to trip Mike up and get him off track.

Mike's patient, humble response astounded me, primarily

because he was still such a young believer at the time. He was clear that he didn't consider himself any kind of biblical scholar. He said simply, "Look, guys, I don't know any of that. I just know that I was blind, and now I see. I know that I was bound up in darkness, but Jesus Christ set me free." Although Mike didn't seem to have a strong grasp of theological matters and -isms, he expressed clearly and humbly that his highest priority was to ensure that his walk with God always remains pure. The level of maturity Mike exhibited that afternoon was further confirmation to me of his sincerity and purity of heart. Mike's certainly not perfect, but he's a man whose life has clearly been completely transformed.

Since that time, I have seen God continue to draw Mike into deeper surrender, brokenness, and freedom in every area of his life—just as He will do for any of His children who approach Him with humility. I am a fan of Mike Leehan. His wholehearted devotion to Christ as his Savior and King is nothing short of inspiring. It's a privilege to call Mike a friend and a prayer partner in our mutual quest to see others become fully devoted followers of Christ.

Jim Kimbrough

The fall of 1994 was a time of transition for me. In the middle of a separation from my wife of eleven years, I was trying to navigate what single life looks like for someone who had been accustomed to marriage. The union had produced no children, and I had to rediscover myself all over again.

Being part of the body of Christ has always been a connection I valued highly, whether in small groups or large gatherings.

Small groups, however, are special and dynamic, places where trust is built and a sense of Christian community is formed. In the context of a small group meeting, I first met Mike.

That night was not particularly special. We had a short message, discussion, and prayer for others. I do remember that Mike was quiet and very observant, eyes wide and darting back and forth. While praying for someone I remember having a sensation of pressure grip my forehead.

When the prayer time was coming to a close, I introduced myself to Mike. He seemed a bit surprised that I would approach him and had a hard time looking me in the eye. I felt as though I had met a friend. I liked Mike. In fact, I felt a strong connection with him. This man would be in my life forever. So I just kept bugging him. I'm sure I was annoying. But Mike graciously entertained me.

Everyone has a story. If we will open our hearts and ears and listen, people have wonderful stories to tell. I love to hear people's stories. I would sit and listen all day to my great-grandmother and her stories of traveling from Texas to Arkansas in a covered wagon, if she would let me. It was no different with Mike. I wanted to know his story if he would trust me enough to tell me.

Mike unfolded a unique story. In the beginning, he spoke to test my ability to hang in there. Would I stay after hearing sordid details of demonic attacks, poltergeist encounters, bloodletting, and the slaying of small animals for sacrificial reasons? To his amazement those stories didn't faze me.

Admittedly, I was a novice at "How do we handle someone who is demon possessed?" or for that matter, "How do we handle someone who is entertaining demons?"

The subject of demons and how to deal with them is not a very comfortable one for American Christians. In fact, the idea that Satan and demons even exist is a subject that some people don't feel they have to entertain. On the other hand, groups exist who think that everything bad can be attributed to demonic activity. Balance is needed here. Little support or information on this subject was available when I was encountering Mike. What little information was available really didn't work for Mike.

It started with my trying during our home group meetings to cast out demons, which Mike could name and/or which could name themselves very well. Mike would end up crouched in a corner of the house with me in his face, shouting at some mysterious creature or creatures to "come out!" Mike's face would contort, he would growl, and I would feel like we were getting somewhere. No one else would help me. The experiences were weird and intimidating.

Feeling underqualified and ill equipped, I was looking for anything that could help Mike. A man in Oklahoma City was being used to minister deliverance to people. So I asked Mike if he wanted to go. He reluctantly agreed. Mike wanted to be free. He was a tormented soul, going back and forth between the door of hell and the door of heaven. God bless him, he was game for just about anything.

We went, listened to the message, and received some material. A man was there to help with deliverance sessions whom I can only describe as the best Elvis impersonator deliverance minister I have ever seen. Between me and Elvis, it didn't take long for things to get out of hand. Mike ended up under a desk somewhere, and I knew that we had lost all control of this situation. It was after this encounter that the Lord spoke to me very clearly: *"Just be Mike's friend."*

By taking the position of Mike's friend, I was giving

responsibility to the Lord for Mike's deliverance. I knew that God would put Mike in the right place and time and with the right people to facilitate his deliverance.

Being Mike's friend can be many things, but it's not boring. Mike thinks and plans. He has an active mind, which must be a blessing and a curse at the same time. I met his three kids when Mike invited me over for lunch. I remember walking up the driveway to see the kids looking out the windows on each side of the front door. When I went in the house, they couldn't keep their eyes off me. Mike shared with me that he had told the kids, "Jim was hit by a bus while riding a skateboard, so don't stare at him." It was so funny.

Mike called one night and said that some creepy things were happening at the house. Suddenly I heard what sounded like a flamethrower, and Mike told me that flames were coming out of his bathroom. I heard eerie speaking sounds in the background as well. These experiences I had to take with a grain of salt. I wasn't impressed. Mike could have duplicated any of those things on the spot. I had heard him make as many as four to five different sounds out of his mouth all at the same time.

Mike went weeks or months at a time without contacting me. When he did call, it was usually associated with a demonic attack. He would tell me that he was in the desert somewhere not knowing how he got there. One time he called when he had driven through Little Rock, Arkansas. A large Pentecostal church off I-40 has a billboard displaying events and service times. He said that he looked up at the sign, and it flashed *"Mike Pull Over."* He did a double take, and it flashed again, *"Mike Pull Over."* He pulled over into the church parking lot and fell asleep. It was Sunday morning. The parking attendants woke him and asked if he wanted to come to church. While there he received some very powerful prayer.

Mike hung out at our little group for a while, and a young man in the group sensed the evil presence that followed Mike and began to do a sort of warfare against him. It looked more like a Jedi trying to use the Force than spiritual warfare. Mike looked at me, I looked at them, and it was comical to say the least.

Mike also predicted, in the midst of clarity, his future in Christ, describing moments of ministry that he and I would engage in. He talked about the books he would write.

About this same time I had met and was beginning to date a young lady named Melissa. I was very transparent to her about my life in God. I shared some of the encounters I was having with Mike. This didn't faze her. We decided to elope. Mike began to disappear more frequently. In one of our contacts, I told him I wanted him to be the best man at our public wedding, which was the first week in August 1995. I couldn't imagine anyone else taking that role but Mike. I knew this was overwhelming to him. I wanted him to know that I loved him. This was my way of showing how much our relationship meant to me.

After the wedding and our honeymoon, Mike became really scarce. In fact, Melissa and I were leaving town to go to Little Rock to see my family when I checked the mail and found a letter return-addressed from the Oklahoma City county jail with Mike's name on it. We went to the jail, and I put my name on the access list and left him some money and a note letting him know that I would contact him when I got back into town.

When he was released from jail, I decided to spend some time with him by buying a bunch of tools and working with him.

I was in the air force at the time and worked a night shift that allowed me some time during the day to do other things. I still have some of those tools! I wasn't a very good assistant, though. I did learn how to put together garage doors. I don't think it was very comforting for the couple that I had to read the instructions to put together their garage door.

I stayed in contact with Mike from time to time. I remember praying that the Lord would put an anchor in Mike's spiritual life so he wouldn't have to deal with the spirit world so much and could work on some of the heart issues that I believe the enemy complicates and takes advantage of.

In June 1998, my first son was born. The same month Trent was born, I received orders to transfer to Biloxi, Mississippi. It was a quick transfer. When we drove into Biloxi the first week in September, we were greeted by Hurricane George. While down in Biloxi, I saw Mike only once. His girlfriend had called me and said that he was in my area and that he wasn't in a good place. Over the years that I have known Mike, I would get a sense of when to call him; I am sure it was the Holy Spirit prompting me. It always seemed to be at the appropriate time. Mike's girlfriend told me the color of his truck and suggested that he might be at a casino. I asked God to show me where Mike was.

I drove out onto the coastal highway, which we lived near, and ventured east. The first casino I came to was The President. I drove into the parking lot and found his truck on the back row. I went into the casino and had two choices, first floor or second floor. I chose the second floor, all the while asking God to direct my steps. When I came off the escalator, I made a beeline to some slot machines. Mike was on the first row, and a chair was available right next to him. I put in a couple of quarters and pulled the lever. I commented out loud something like, "Man, these things are a rip-off!" He looked over, and his eyes got as big as half-dollars. We had a chance to talk. He was describing what he was up to, and I pleaded with him not to go. He was doing something in Florida, and I felt no peace in my spirit about this trip.

I didn't hear from Mike much until we returned from Biloxi in 2003. I had been praying about a house to move into but had received no direction or feedback from anyone I had asked. I contacted Mike on a Monday. We were supposed to leave on Thursday. Mike and his now ex-girlfriend are both generous people, and the house where they met was still not rented, so they allowed us to move in there.

During this time, Mike was really struggling with whether God was good or evil. Did He even exist? He was reaching a real boiling point. I couldn't help him with this. I knew it would take a personal encounter with the living God to bring him around. He called me in the winter of 2007 and said he had been hanging out with a bunch of guys. They had asked him to go to a men's retreat. He decided to go at the last minute, and the rest is history.

Because I had seen this glimmer of hope in his eyes from time to time, it took me about two weeks to realize the encounter was the real deal. At this writing, it has been three years since his salvation. I had never seen Mike cry . . . ever! Now his heart is tender. He is teachable and repentant. The moment he realizes he is going against love, he is quick to repent.

The blood of Christ and work of the cross is complete. God is bigger; Satan's a liar and defeated. We are here on earth to glorify the Lord and demonstrate that defeat.

I want to thank the Lord Jesus Christ of Nazareth for pouring

His love out to my friend Mike. Thank You for answering our and his prayers. God is good all the time, and His mercy endures forever!

I mentioned earlier that when Mike had his "mountaintop" experience, it took me a few weeks to realize that this was the moment we both knew would come. The kind of life Mike was living was so volatile that I knew it would lead to death one day unless the Lord was determined to keep him alive. If the Lord determined to keep him alive, then it was for a purpose. Since that day never came, God has a plan for him to stick around.

Today, my brother is ministering practically every day and every hour of the day. This is a man consumed with passion for Jesus and seeing people set free. Free from sin and apathy and free to pursue their destiny in God. This doesn't surprise me. I knew that when Mike finally gave control of his life over to his Savior, he would be a firebrand. What has surprised me, and it really shouldn't have, is the level of persecution that he has received from the church—people who call themselves "Christians." Then, that may be the problem. There is a big difference between a Christian and a Christ follower. Some people think they are Christian by birth, some by relationship, and some just because there is loose affiliation with Jesus.

One of the things I've seen Mike do, with great passion, is listen to the voice of his Shepherd. Mike loves Jesus, and it shows. He is used mightily by God to speak into people's lives. Mike has surrounded himself with an amazing faith community. It is a community of trust where freedom and personal responsibility are practiced. In an environment of freedom, there has to be confrontation. Confrontation is not conflict; it is, however, designed to strengthen and to teach.

Some call Mike a prophet. I just call him a normal Christian. He's just doing the things that normal Christians should be doing. He is an example of what God wants to do through the body of Christ. One of the jobs of an Old Testament prophet was to call God's people back into covenant relationship. I see this happening through Mike as well. Through Mike's ministry, God is calling His people, His bride, to purity. The pure in heart shall see God.

Michael Hoang

I first met Mike Leehan when he spoke at Bushido, a men's retreat with LifeChurch.tv. The minute I heard our guest speaker was an ex-satanist, I began texting my friends in the area to get them to come. As he gave his testimony about his ascent from darkness, I was instantly captivated by his story. How did someone so deep into the evil and darkness of satanism become someone so on fire and passionate about the Lord? The contrast between his struggle with satanism and his experience of Christianity was striking.

After his testimony, Mike opened for questions from the audience. I couldn't help but raise my hand. The questions he answered kept bringing to mind new questions. People really worship and call on demons? What do demons look like? How do they attack us? Question after question raced through my mind. Unfortunately, our time was cut short. I could have talked to this guy all night! His testimony really opened up my eyes to how real and present the unseen spiritual world is.

After the retreat, I got Mike's phone number from a staff member who had put the weekend together. I was hoping to sit down with him and ask him some more questions about his experiences on the dark side. I've had various supernatural occurrences in my life that I have never really understood and was hoping he could shine some light into them.

I finally called him, and he welcomed the opportunity to get together. A friend and I met him at Panera Bread in Edmond. As we talked, I realized he was unlike anyone I'd ever talked to before! In his life, the supernatural was normal. Things I'd only heard about were an everyday thing for him. You can literally hear and be led by the Holy Spirit? Spiritual gifts? Prophecy? Though I had experienced a lot in my Christian walk (or so I thought at the time), I was a bit skeptical. But my thirst for knowledge and understanding kept drawing me in. We sat and talked for hours. Could this all be real? My mind was expanding. After we left, I couldn't stop thinking and talking to others about what I was hearing.

The next week, we met back up at the prayer chapel at the Edmond LifeChurch campus, this time with a dozen other friends we had talked to. We talked and took turns asking questions about his testimony, the dark side, and the Holy Spirit. After a long time of talking, we all prayed as a group—and boy, did God show up! We all felt the power of the Holy Spirit in an unexplainable way. As we were praying, I remember feeling a gentle weight and warmth all around me like I was wearing fifteen fur coats. Mike turned to me and told me he was seeing a beam of light coming down on me from heaven. We were all in awe of the reality of God's presence. I'd been a Christian for so long, and I'd never really heard about this stuff. It was like I was walking around my old familiar house that I've lived in my whole life and I stumbled upon a little door. I opened it, and behind that door was this *enormous* gymnasium I never knew was there!

After we all left, I couldn't stop thinking about the night. My mind was racing. I needed to talk to someone about this! I drove half an hour to a small group where some of us who were at the prayer chapel had gone. We walked in without a word, but everyone knew something was going on. They could feel it. When asked what was going on, we could not stop talking! I felt like we were the shepherds after they saw baby Jesus for the first time. We had to tell somebody! We all grew that day. Our spiritual eyes were starting to be opened. Was this what Acts 2 was like? Everything felt so new, so fresh, so real again—like seeing the world as a new Christian. Needless to say, the next week, our prayer chapel group doubled.

Since then, Mike and I have become good friends. He has incredible spiritual gifts and is one of the few people I know who is really walking out his faith. Through our friendship and his mentorship, I have learned a great deal about the spiritual world and have matured in my Christian faith. I see God noticeably moving around him all the time to transform hundreds of lives around Edmond, Oklahoma. To see the fruit of a man who has been on fire for God for just a few years is amazing! God will lead him to do something, and he just does it. He's not anything special; he's simply a guy who has seen what's on the other side and has now fully committed to the side of Christ.

Kathy Hayes

Knowing Mike Leehan has changed my life. My husband and I met Mike about a year and a half ago. He comes to our life group when he can. It is always different when he is there. Because of his past, and his coming out of satanism, he has a much deeper relationship with the Lord.

Mike is very charismatic. He can "read" people. Sometimes the Lord gives him a special knowledge about where a person is at in life. I know when he does this it is right on. The person gets confirmation because God has already been talking to him, and Mike's words are the confirmation. I have seen this again and again. Mike is constantly ministering because there are so many people who are desperate to hear from God, but their sin, immaturity, or whatever blocks them from hearing. Also, the Lord uses Mike to lead people to salvation. He is awesome in dealing with people who feel that they have sinned too much for God to forgive. He has the heart of his Father. He knows he is forgiven, but he never forgets where he's been. This makes him incredibly powerful in the spiritual realm.

In my own life, Mike makes me want to press in to the Lord more. I see the Lord using him, and I want to be a better vessel. He is so dedicated. He knows what it means to die to oneself. He has given it all to the Lord. He puts his own needs second to serving the Lord. Ministering is a timely job. The pay is rare, but the heavenly benefits are awesome.

This book is a God deal. I am convinced that Mike's story will draw many people to the Lord. Satan tried to steal, take over, and destroy a life and did for a time . . . but then Mike gave his life to the Lord. When someone who is deep into Satan turns to God, there is no lukewarm playing around. Mike realizes what is at stake and lays his life down before the Lord every day. He isn't interested in becoming famous for his own glory—he wants to glorify the Lord. The adversary is constantly trying to make Mike stumble, but he keeps pressing on and pressing in to the Lord, despite challenges and even several attempts on his life.

The witness he gives to the Lord is huge. Mike is focused. His life is all about Jesus. He has a heart for the lost. He tells it like it is.

If there is something big going on in my life and I am desperate to hear from the Lord, I call Mike and ask him to pray. I know the Father hears me, but it seems like Mike has a more direct line of communication through prayer than I do. I have seen pastors call him when they are dealing with a situation that seems hopeless. Mike doesn't blink an eye at what the world looks at as hopeless. The love of the Lord flows through him. It is an honor to be a part of Mike's life.

George Clark

I am convinced that many of the "lucky breaks" in life are directed rather than happenstance. It's the delays at home only to find out that there was an accident on the highway you just missed or some other obstruction. Moments of frustration can often lead to a sigh of relief later. So we walk out our annoyances trusting that God is actively working in our lives. This extends to "chance" meetings with people.

I'm still not sure how exactly I met Mike. Knowing one person led to meeting another person who recommended a Bible study, which led me to another group and landed me in a prayer meeting. I watched Mike speak to the group with great discernment and God-given knowledge. It wasn't like watching a pastor's sermon on Sunday; it was more akin to a spiritual surgeon pinpointing cancer. One guy walked into the meeting late and was immediately met with, "So who's the woman you really ticked off?" There is no hiding with Mike. But God has given Mike a character I can trust.

I've never encountered anyone who delved that far into the satanic. His story opened my eyes not only to the occult but to the constant spiritual battles around us. God has used Mike to provide invaluable wisdom in my life.

I've had the opportunity to spend time with Jim Kimbrough, Mike, David Barnes, and Joe Thomas. Between hearing the story of the time they bumped into twelve satanists while at a restaurant and the story of cultists leaving dead snakes and crows on Mike's doorstep, I've had the opportunity to get used to the weird.

What has been the greatest asset isn't listening to these stories; it has been Mike's mentorship. He has always been direct and on point with me. Reading his story has opened my eyes to a side of spirituality I never even considered. That may seem odd to say at first. But realize that most in the United States think that the devil is a contraption of Hollywood and that dark entities always end up with someone's head spinning around spewing pea soup. My generation and the one following me grew up with zombie movies and overly grotesque slasher films. More spiritual things are left to those with mental illnesses hearing voices while high on drugs or something. We forget those precious words from Ephesians 6—we deal with principalities and powers.

I would not have believed many of the stories in this book had I not met Mike and had the blessing of spending time with him. I've spoken with those who knew him before Christ and after Christ. The accounts are consistent.